SÉAMUS BRENNAN

SÉAMUS BRENNAN

A Life in Government

Frank Lahiffe

The Liffey Press

Published by
The Liffey Press
Ashbrook House, 10 Main Street
Raheny, Dublin 5, Ireland
www.theliffeypress.com

A catalogue record of this book is
available from the British Library.

ISBN 978-1-905785-63-6

The early photographs in this book are from the personal collection of
the late Tess Brennan, while the official pictures are courtesy of Maxwell
Photography, Dargle House, 98 Lower Drumcondra Road, Dublin 9.

Printed in the United Kingdom by Athenaeum Press.

Contents

Foreword

THIS FIRST BOOK ABOUT SÉAMUS BRENNAN is unlikely to be the last word, but it is a timely and excellent appraisal of the public life of a gifted politician and charming man. It is fitting that in his first biographer, Séamus has again found the service of his long-time adviser and friend, Frank Lahiffe. Frank was a close associate of Séamus during many of the events described and is one of those in politics and in life who knew him best.

I first met Séamus Brennan in Moran's Hotel on Talbot Street in 1973. He was already a political prodigy having at the age of 25 been appointed General Secretary of Fianna Fáil by Jack Lynch that year. If many bright young men and women have enjoyed a promising start in politics, very few have successfully survived the subsequent winnowing of events as Séamus did. Indeed, even before he was entrusted with national responsibility by Jack Lynch, he had already enjoyed the experience of student politics at University College Galway.

Born in 1948 and growing up in the 1950s and 1960s, Séamus personified all his life a belief in modernisation that was resonant of the era when he came of age. The arrival of prosperity, the advent of television, and the great advances in technology that characterized the 1960s are all clearly strands in the great man the young boy grew up to become. Our modern Ireland took root and grew up out of that time. If its origins were a legacy of older men like Seán Lemass and T.K. Whitaker, it was seized upon by a younger generation of whom Séamus proved to be among the most influential and enduring. Séamus grew up to believe that things could be different and he set out to make sure that they were. Years later, during the dark times of the 1980s, when progress seemed to be past and prosperity only a pipe dream, Séamus stood out as somebody who had a profound belief in politics as an agent of change. He was never there to manage the status quo – for him the present was only ever a preface to progress.

In public life, he was both an innovator and an achiever. He not only believed in politics but he hugely enjoyed it too. The general election of 1977 marked a new departure in campaigning as Séamus brought showmanship to the hustings and made elections more interesting events. The black and white images of an older style of politics were replaced with the colour Séamus innovated in public life.

The aftermath of the famous victory brought him into the Oireachtas as a Senator, and in 1981 he was elected to Dáil Éireann on the first of nine successive occasions.

I was part of the unexpected and thitherto unknown Fianna Fáil majority that was swept into Leinster House in 1977. Séamus was already a nationally known figure and destined for greater things. As so often happens in politics, the tectonic plates shifted. An economic downturn in the country, a change of leadership in the party, and a time of unprecedented internal strife in Fianna Fáil tested the mettle of a young man who thus far had enjoyed a charmed political life. Out of real adversity, a tough, wise and determined Séamus Brennan emerged. He was determined to stick the course of turbulent events and to make his contribution to national life and he did.

He and I served together as ministers in every Fianna Fáil-led Government from 1987 until my retirement as Taoiseach in 2008. In the event, my own departure was his cue to step aside and make one last and mighty stand against the illness that threatened to lay him low. Even as he fought that last campaign with mortality, he came out onto the hustings to support a Yes vote in the Lisbon referendum. He understood that Europe was an integral part of Irish progress. He had lived and led the changes that our membership had brought over 30 years. Our membership of the European Union coincided almost exactly with his own career in public life. It rhymed exactly with his passion for change. In its physical bravery, that last campaign was of a piece with the political leader I knew and admired. He was utterly undeterred by events and completely at home on the hustings. He was from beginning to end one of the great Irish political campaigners. And in the end, his last act was to continue campaigning for what he believed.

Frank Lahiffe's book recalls the range of ministerial experiences, the politics and the policies that Séamus was part of. As a colleague and as Taoiseach, I can recall vividly his incisive analysis and contribution to a broad swathe of policy over several decades. The growth of modern Irish aviation is largely due to the two airline policy he pioneered in 1989. It was a pillar of much of our subsequent economic opportunity. As Minister for Commerce, he championed small business and enabling entrepreneurship.

I especially remember with profound gratitude and real admiration the role he played as Chief Whip from 1997 to 2002. When it was formed in June 1997, that minority government, which achieved so much for peace and prosperity, was not expected to last until Christmas. In fact, it was the first Coalition Government in Irish political history to run its full course of five years. Séamus's innate political skill as Chief Whip was an integral and essential part of the success of that administration. His subsequent and brilliant daily delivery for Fianna Fáil of the campaign "A Lot Done, More To Do" during the general election of 2002 was vintage Séamus.

He was proud of his family and they of him. Their private grief for the loss of a public man is I hope assuaged by the good he did and the legacy he has left. I never knew another private man apart from the gracious public figure. In good times and in bad, he was composed, courteous and generous to all.

If as a politician he was gifted with talent, as a man he was defined by charm and courtesy. In the political world, where the oxygen is thin and events are disconcerting, few kept their composure as completely as Séamus Brennan did.

For more than 30 years, I was privileged to know and work with Séamus Brennan. He is gone, but his legacy lives on. In a real sense, it is the same cause he rallied to as a young man. It is a vision of an Ireland that can change for the better, that can foster talent and provide opportunity, and where the present is only ever a preface to progress.

Bertie Ahern TD
Former Taoiseach

This book is dedicated to Anne and Darina Lahiffe, my wife and daughter, who kept the home fires burning while quietly enduring my long working days and nights which entailed office work, meetings and travel – all prerequisites for a person working at any political level – while I followed my own political path and dreams with my good friend and professional colleague, Séamus Brennan. Without their support and understanding, my life with Séamus in Government would not have been possible – nor indeed would it have been possible to write this book.

Chapter 1

The Early Years –
An Introduction to Politics

THE IRELAND THAT IRISH PEOPLE ALL over the world know and love changed dramatically over the period from 1987 to 2008 – a time when I had the honour of working professionally with a person described variously as a "wonderful statesman", and "an exceptional politician". That person was Séamus Brennan.

Séamus Eugene Brennan (1948–2008) was described by many people during his lifetime and, more significantly perhaps, after his death as "a master politician". And that he was. He had the common touch. He instinctively knew how people felt and what they thought. He could relate to them. In an article entitled "Famously Séamus" which appeared in The Sunday Business Post Online (ThePost.ie), writer Niamh Connolly said that he "inspires a heady mix of admiration, dislike, envy and jealousy from his colleagues in Government". On an RTÉ Prime Time interview with Séamus and former Labour Party Leader Pat Rabbitte, the latter said that Séamus had a "wide-eyed innocent look", a comment which was perceived within political circles as possible envy at his high profile which may go back to Galway University days when Séamus beat Pat Rabbitte in student elections – also a time when former Labour Party Minister, Michael D. Higgins, was one of their lecturers.

Growing up in Devon Park in Salthill, Galway was something which Séamus never lost sight of. He was immensely proud of his Galway heritage throughout his life. His father James had come to

Galway as a young man but was born on the 45 acres Clawinch Island, Co. Longford, in the scenic Lough Ree, close to the Roscommon shore and 14 miles north of Athlone. Clawinch Island (some mistakenly spell it as Claunch) had 25 acres of good grazing with the remainder mainly woodland and scrub. It was accessible only by boat with just two landing places on the east and west shores. Séamus's mother, Tess O'Donnell, was born in Clonavenden, Ballintubber, Co. Roscommon and was reared in Castle Street, Roscommon. As a result of this mixed geographical pedigree, Séamus was fond of telling people that he not only came from Galway, but from Roscommon and Longford as well. As you can imagine, this went down particularly well when he was visiting those areas.

He was one of five children in the Brennan household – four boys (Joe, Séamus, Eamonn and Terry) and one girl (Carmel). His father was a small builder, responsible for the construction of two Galway churches – St. Patrick's in Forster Street and the church in Barna – while also building an extension to their own local Church of Christ the King in Salthill. During his building career, he also carried out works at eight schools in Galway City and County, along with the former Roches Stores and houses in Kingston, Salthill, The Crescent and two houses at Devon Park, including the family home. Meanwhile, Séamus's mother had a small guest house. When not engaged in building work, Séamus's father was active in Galway Fianna Fáil circles, serving as Director of Elections in the 1960s, among other roles, and it has been said in Galway that the political gene cultivated by his father was the catalyst for Séamus to become involved in politics himself, which he did from his teenage years.

From early schooldays at Scoil Fhursa and St. Patrick's National School in Salthill, Séamus went on to secondary school at St. Joseph's ("The Bish" as it is called) before moving on to University College Galway where he graduated with a B.Comm and a B.A. (Econ.) and became an accountant (subsequently achieving an M.Comm at University College Dublin). He often told the story of how he ended up as an accountant:

Back in the days when all you needed to go to university (apart from the fees) were a couple of Honours in your Leaving Certificate, a group of us were after getting our Leaving Certificate results and were sitting on a wall, discussing what course we should do. We were looking at all the options and some of us read about the Commerce course and felt that it would be good, and might make us a bit of money. And so we signed up for it. Others in the group signed up for various other subjects, and that quire simply is how I ended up studying for my B.Comm.

The veteran former TD, Minister and Member of the European Parliament, Mark Killilea, has claimed credit for Séamus getting on the first rung of what was an extraordinary political ladder – the National Executive or Ard Comhairle of Fianna Fáil. Séamus had contested what is known as the Committee of 15 election for the National Executive (where the electorate is composed of Ard Fheis delegates from all over Ireland) but in the only election defeat of his career, he was not victorious. Mark Killilea takes up the story: "I proposed at a meeting that Séamus Brennan be co-opted to the Ard Comhairle and my proposal was accepted." Thus began a truly extraordinary political career which would ultimately result in a whole generation of Irish political history being changed.

After marriage to Ann O'Shaughnessy, who shared his Roscommon roots, they had six children – two boys (Shay and Eanna) and four girls (Daire, Aoife, Breffni and Sine). On moving to Dublin, his first home was at Glendoher, Rathfarnham, before moving to Hollywood Drive, Goatstown and finally to Finsbury Park, Churchtown.

His eternal resting place is in St. Nathi's Cemetary, midway between his home at Finsbury Park in Churchtown and his beloved Dundrum Luas Bridge.

Within his closest political circle, he was known simply as "SB", but to his constituents he always wanted to be known as "Séamus", and throughout his political life made a point of specifically asking them not to refer to him as "Minister" or "Mr. Brennan". Similarly, letters to constituents were always signed as "Séamus". This "man of the people" trait saw him returned to Dáil Éireann at the top of the poll on several occasions, but never out of the first couple of seats filled during his nine general election campaigns, and one Local Election campaign.

He was a great listener. It was impossible to have a disagreement with him because of his very gentle manner which would never see him embroiled in argument, or even raise his voice. Senator Dan Boyle of the Green Party put it like this:

> During negotiations to agree the Programme for Government, Séamus was always on hand to try to bring people together when voices were raised and tempers became more heated than they should have been. It was his nature to accept a political argument, never to react to belligerence and never to seek to deny the right of others to make an argument. These were among his greatest political strengths.

His trademark smile was often called "the biggest smile in Leinster House".

In Séamus's world, everyone had a point of view and no opposing view was ever shot down by personal attacks or because someone had an opposite view. Calmly arguing his point of view and winning people over to his convictions was his hallmark – and a great gift for a politician to have. He often said, quite jokingly, that he "would love to have a Yes Man" as his professional and voluntary advisers were renowned for speaking out to him whenever they disagreed with an approach he was taking. But of course, if everyone had agreed with him all the time, he would have hated it.

In a commentary in the *Irish Independent* following his untimely death, author and political columnist John Cooney wrote about meeting Séamus over the years for various briefings when he:

> ... projected an air of mystery as a deep thinker about the nature of Irish society and its future cultural

development. By implication, he conveyed the impression that his innate ambition and natural abilities made him a 'man of destiny' who would be a doer, a man of action, if only he were given the political power to do so.

He went on to suggest that Séamus was:

strangely imitative of Charles J. Haughey in speech, walk and mannerisms ... stirring his cup of coffee or tea with a spoon in the same leisurely and reflective way that 'the Boss' would often do, to give greater emphasis to his utterances.

Séamus had a tremendous wit and in any discussion about anything, no matter how heated the debate or conversation became, he could always be relied upon to bring humour to the situation, often disarming political opponents in the process – which used to drive them nuts because his opponents found it so hard to land a punch. As an astute, capable and experienced politician and minister, his ability was way beyond question throughout the many roles in which he served with great distinction. In one of his nine general election campaigns, his poster and canvass literature proudly proclaimed, "Proven Ability at a National Level".

Throughout his professional political career from the age of 25, when he was appointed as General Secretary of Fianna Fáil by Jack Lynch, he was seen as a visionary. Taoiseach Brian Cowen would later describe him as "an inspired choice". But the former minister and long time Fianna Fáil TD, Dr. Michael Woods, who was heavily involved in the selection process for what he called "a dynamic person" to succeed Tommy Mullins as General Secretary, recalls discussing the job specification with Jack Lynch and others at the time: "Fianna Fáil was operating on a shoestring but we needed to develop the Party. We needed a real go-getter." The serious political force that Fianna Fáil had been under de Valera, Lemass and Lynch in the earlier years had been severely tested by the beginning of the Northern Ireland "troubles" and the Republic's response to the civil, religious and political conflict of that time. Jack Lynch was just the third leader of Fianna Fáil when he was elected in 1966 but later achieved the reputation of being "the real Taoiseach", a description which was to rankle with his immediate successor, Charlie Haughey.

Jack Lynch was great for spotting emerging talent and apart from his wisdom in recruiting a young Séamus Brennan as General Secretary of Fianna Fáil, he was always on the lookout for possible new members. One who came across his radar was Eoin O'Brien whom he had met at a social function. Jack arranged for his new General Secretary to contact Eoin and the two met for the first time at Larry Murphy's pub on Dublin's Lower Baggot Street in 1973. Striking up a friendship from the beginning, Eoin was quickly encouraged to become a member of the party and joined a Cumann in Dublin Central Constituency, before transferring some years later to a Cumann in Séamus's own Dublin South. Eoin would later be a key person in the future Brennan election machine, serving as Séamus's personal Director of Elections on several occasions.

As General Secretary, one of Séamus's duties was to make a weekly visit to the former President and founding father of Fianna Fáil, Eamon de Valera, at Linden Convalescent Home in Blackrock, a stone's throw from the former de Valera home on Cross Avenue opposite the back entrance to Dev's alma mater, Blackrock College. Dev had specifically asked to be kept informed and up to date on what was happening in Fianna Fáil, and while he was effectively blind, de Valera's mind was still very sharp and enquiring, according to Séamus. And it was a task that Séamus felt very privileged to do.

A motion from the 1974 Ard Fheis would be the spur for the establishment of Ogra Fianna Fáil – a specific youth body within the Fianna Fáil umbrella – a project which Séamus felt very much at home with. The motion, which had Séamus's full support, asked for youth to be given a say in the future of Fianna Fáil. To its credit, Fianna Fáil was the first political party to recognise that young people had a voice which needed to be heard and it there-fore fell to its youthful General Secretary, Séamus Brennan, to put the plans into action. He laid it clearly on the table that "for a party with such a record, it has not succeeded in bringing in (to politics) its quota of idealistic and motivated young people", and he was determined to change that.

The first National Youth Conference was held in Dublin's Bur-lington Hotel in January 1975 with three key aims: to establish the views of Fianna Fáil's young people, to show the public that Fi-anna Fáil had a commitment to youth, and to pursue more youth involvement in the Party. Ogra Fianna Fáil continued to rapidly develop after that and the effectiveness of the policy has been shown over the years with an increasing number of younger peo-ple offering themselves for election to internal Fianna Fáil posts, as well as in local and national elections, where many have subse-quently assumed ministerial roles. It also helped to develop the political ideas of young people who wanted to work outside politi-cal life, and one of those was the late Veronica Guerin, who bravely took on the criminal underworld through her writings in the *Sunday Independent* and gave her life when she was gunned down on the Naas Road near the Dublin suburb of Clondalkin.

Continually seeking to develop new ideas for political cam-paigning, Séamus was credited by political peers of all persuasions with what the *Connacht Tribune* called "reshaping the whole land-scape of elections in Ireland". The fascination for new and innova-tive ideas first surfaced when he went to check out the political campaign of President Jimmy Carter in America in 1976. On that trip, he also met with American media guru, David Garth, at his office on New York's Fifth Avenue. He was accompanied by his long time friend, Bob Manson Sr., who had once been a local elec-tion candidate himself in Dublin North-East, and had begun his own political life as a close associate of former Fianna Fáil Tanaiste, George Colley.

The intelligence gathered at that time was to have a dramatic effect on the 1977 general election when Jack Lynch gave Séamus a free rein to campaign in a new way. Ireland had never seen anything like it – presidential-style campaigning, marketing strategies, opinion polls, a slogan – "Bring Back Jack" – and a specially commissioned song, "Your Kind of Country", which was sung by Colm C.T. Wilkinson. The former Dublin Member of the European Parliament, Eoin Ryan, recalled his late father, Senator Eoin Ryan (one of the elder statesmen in Fianna Fáil, and a son of Dr. James Ryan, one of the founders of the party and a former minister) discussing this new fangled idea for a pop song and you can just imagine the varied thoughts going through the respective heads of the senior politician and the youthful General Secretary in relation to their own choices of music. But the song had mass appeal outside of its role in the political world and subsequently became a chart hit.

The electorate responded with gusto to all these new ideas by giving Fianna Fáil its famous 20 seat majority, helped also by the innovative policies announced during the campaign, including the removal of the motor tax and the abolition of domestic rates. While Séamus always stoutly defended the innovative policies of that period, not everyone in his circle held the same view. Eoin O'Brien recalls advising Séamus to "phase in the new policies" rather than going at them hell for leather. While the motor tax has since come back, and there is talk of domestic rates doing likewise in some shape or form, Séamus remained unapologetic for promoting what was an exceptionally brave idea at the time to remove what was seen as an unfair tax as it took no account of ability to pay. A generation of householders have every reason to thank Séamus for the vision he showed because if domestic rates were still around in their old form, it is likely that the charge would be many thousands of euro annually.

A little known story, told by Andrew Lynch in the *Evening Herald*, depicts Séamus on the morning of the election result in his living room in Goatstown, "jumping around with excitement dressed only in his underpants".

In later years, under Charlie Haughey, Séamus wanted to again put razzmatazz into the campaign and brought updated ideas to P.J. Mara, who was a close associate of Charlie. The expectation was that P.J. would pass on the suggestions, but according to a close associate of Séamus who was present at the time, "P.J. did not appear to pass on the information or Charlie did not take account of it". Whatever happened, this associate told of his strong opinion that P.J. did not want Séamus to get credit for any electoral innovations. But Mara was known to be quite generous in his praise for Séamus in later years, and probably respected what Séamus had achieved. He often spoke humorously of Séamus's appetite for "global domination", and his biography by Tim Ryan, published in 1992, quoted him as saying that "Séamus Brennan is a politician who has achieved a lot for Fianna Fáil ... I think an economic posting might suit him".

An interesting footnote is that when Séamus was elected to the Dáil in 1981, he automatically resigned from the Seanad seat he had occupied since 1977, although the outgoing Seanad still had six weeks or so to go until the new one came into being. As Séamus had been Taoiseach Jack Lynch's nominee in 1977, it fell to the then Taoiseach, Charlie Haughey, to fill the vacancy for the remainder of the outgoing Seanad. Who did Charlie appoint? None other than one P.J. Mara!

The schedule of Séamus's working day was often so extensive that he would forget to eat regularly – hardly surprising when a cursory look at a typical ministerial diary in his collection showed 1,100 inside and outside formal engagements in a 12 months period, including the traditional holiday period of August, which really gives the lie to media stories that ministers go on holiday each time the Dáil adjourns. If he found that he had a down moment and time to think, he would say to one of his aides, "Would you like to go for a rasher?" Very often, the "rasher" might be code for a bowl of soup, or bacon and cabbage, or just a fruit scone – but it became a standard saying among his personal staff which signified that he needed to go for food, and invariably it would be a working break with an adviser. He had a particular fondness for fresh fruit, and if one of his staff happened to leave an apple or a banana lying around, he would ask if it was going bad. Invariably, the staff member concerned would say yes and the apple or banana would be in Séamus's hand as he strolled happily back to his own office.

Although Séamus described himself as an economist because of his business training, and was an avid reader of *The Economist* magazine, he was highly critical of so called modern economists for not forecasting the Celtic Tiger. In an address to the Patrick MacGill Summer School in Glenties, Co. Donegal in June 2005, he gave his frank thoughts on economists and on Ireland as it was then:

> Indulging in crystal ball gazing for politicians is, to say the least, a precarious business. And not just for politicians. Search as I might, I have still to find an economist or economic commentator who forecast the economic surge delivered by the Celtic Tiger.
>
> So, for my own part, perhaps the best way to approach the issue is to draw on my own experiences, fashioned out of 25 years or more in national politics, to pose, and attempt to answer, a few fundamental questions. How did Ireland reach so quickly the elevated position it now enjoys? What is this confident, swaggering Ireland achieving? And, most important of all, what does the future hold in store for a country that has changed, changed utterly, inside a relatively few years?
>
> It is fair to say that I have journeyed together with this country through its trials, tribulations and triumphs over the past 30 years or more. At the age of 25, I was thrust into the front line of national politics as General Secretary of Fianna Fáil, then under the solid guardianship of Jack Lynch. My passion for politics, and a love of seeing democracy working to try and improve the lot of all the people, has swept me along on the highs of witnessing the new, vibrant Ireland emerging from the gloom of emigration and recession.

It has hardened me to the consequences of the politics of intransigence when coalition in Government was a dirty word; we in Fianna Fáil fought three general elections in 18 months, and also fought each other, in a vain attempt, and in the teeth of growing reality, to preserve a one party Government system. It has taken me into the furnace of political intrigue. Above all else, it has taught me a lot. I've made mistakes and I've learned by my mistakes. The same as along the way, I believe, this country has learned by its mistakes.

I take particular pride in having been a witness, sometimes in Government, sometimes not, to Ireland as it got into its stride. Seeing a country change before your eyes, watching the metamorphosis from grey, colourless, repressive and drab into an explosion of colour, life, expression and vibrancy has been an exhilarating experience."

One of the burning issues over his time in Government was the concept of social partnership, where unions, employers, Government and other "representative" groups meet at regular intervals to discuss pay and other issues in the workplace, in return for industrial peace. The concept was originally put in place by Charlie Haughey, but Séamus confided to a number of close associates that despite its many positive aspects, he had some difficulties with it. He passionately believed that a Government elected with an agreed programme is much more democratic and open than one negotiating issues behind closed doors with groups who were not necessarily democratically representative of their particular sectors. But he recognised that the side benefit of negotiating on pay issues, which was designed to avoid disputes in the workplace, was useful. And the system was in place, so he was going to use it when required despite his personal views. Of course, his views on giving trade unions the power to directly influence Government thinking were doubtless coloured by the experiences he had in various ministries when trying to introduce reforms.

Apart from well recognised political and numeric abilities, Séamus bore a similarity to Garret FitzGerald and Bertie Ahern in a more unusual way – his choice of an article of clothing. In Garret's case, he was famously caught out wearing two odd shoes. But in Bertie's case, a Dublin South constituent loves to tell people of a time when she was attending a function in Dublin at which Bertie was the guest of honour, and she pointed out to him that he was wearing two odd socks, something he used to recall himself when meeting her at other functions in later years. And there was the time when Bertie was attending the official opening of a mosque in Clonskeagh in Séamus's constituency. Entry to the mosque required the removal of footwear and before he arrived, the question was asked half jokingly but fully in earnest if he would have a hole in his socks – but he didn't on that occasion.

In Séamus's case, it was his use of an old long, blue and belted raincoat which had seen better days – a bit like the well told stories about Bertie Ahern's attachment to an old anorak! As it was proving difficult to part Séamus from this apparently beloved raincoat, it was decided that the coat would have to be hidden to encourage him to forget about it – the plan worked and the coat was subsequently officially retired to a safe place and disposed of at a later date.

Prior to the 1997 general election, Séamus was again thinking internationally and introduced Bertie Ahern to the idea of using political consultants. The firm of Shrum, Devine & Donilon was identified and checked out – Bob Shrum, Tad Devine and Mike Donilon had a successful track record in a number of US presidential campaigns together with general elections in a number of countries. This time, expert advice was going to be taken and the firm was to prove decisive in generating newer models of campaigning for the Fianna Fáil hat trick at the 1997, 2002 and 2007 general elections.

The political vision that Séamus showed and the ability to think outside traditional structures served him well in bringing fresh insights into the remarkable range of Government roles which he uniquely fulfilled. He was greatly helped in both his political and Government roles by being the clear beneficiary of exceptional loyalty from those around him, whether they were professional personal staff, civil servants, close friends, political volunteers, constituents or his official drivers over the years. Writing in the *Mayo News* after his death, Liamy MacNally said that "such loyalty can never be bought, just as it can never be captured in words".

Indeed, without his drivers, some of whom only served for short periods, life would have been much more difficult and they deserve special mention: Tony Boyle, Joe Callinan, Tom Collins, Jackie Dolan, Bill Duggan, Liam Farrell, Andy Kilfeather, Val Lynn, Dermot McCormack, Malachy Mannion, Pat Morris and Peter O'Grady. Between them, coming from various parts of Ireland, they represented a great swathe of Irish geography and were a fount of knowledge as Séamus made his way around Ireland on official business.

But without his original and special political machine, he could not have achieved his goals. The Sunday Business Post Online (ThePost.ie) had a quote from an unnamed political pundit in a piece written by Niamh Connolly on 1 December 2002:

> Brennan runs a brilliant constituency organisation, probably the best after Bertie Ahern's. Dublin South is known as a highly volatile constituency with a history of high profile ministers in shock departures. It's a very big constituency with fickle middle-class voters, but Brennan usually tops the poll.

"Omnipresence" was a catchword authored by Bob Manson Sr. It represented the need for Séamus to be seen everywhere in order to have political success, and it became a much-used word in the constituency organisation at each election time in particular. Wherever he travelled on official business, whether in Ireland or overseas, it was remarkable how often he came across people with links to his constituency. Never failing to use these opportunities to establish where in the constituency the link was, he always made a mental note of the information which would later be put on his constituency records to recall for another occasion. This again proved the truth of the quote attributed to the US Speaker of the House of Representatives, Tip O'Neill, that "all politics is local" – he was explaining how the problems and concerns of towns and cities around the country affect the actions of their representatives – and went on to say:

> I have been in politics all my life. I am proud to be a politician. No other career affords as much opportunity to help people. Let us not concern ourselves with what we have tried and failed, but with what it is still possible to do. Let us spare no energy that the nation and the world may be better for our efforts.

That could very well be a fitting epitaph for Séamus.

There were so many incidents and events over the 21 years that it would take a whole series of books to chronicle them all. A Google or a Yahoo search of "Séamus Brennan" or "Minister Séamus Brennan" inevitably turns up tens of thousands of references. But for a former Minister for Arts and Sport, it is somewhat poignant that on the website www.lastingtribute.co.uk, Séamus is surrounded by folk singer Ronnie Drew, footballer Dermot Curtis and singer Joe Dolan, who all died between December 2007 and November 2008.

Without doubt, Séamus Brennan really did alter the course of a generation in Ireland's political and social landscape. He was an extraordinary person, whose mould was broken when he was created and the like of him will not be seen again.

"A nation reveals itself not only by the men it produces but also by the men it honours, the men it remembers", President John F. Kennedy said of the poet Robert Frost, quoted by An Taoiseach, Brian Cowen at the funeral of Séamus Brennan, 11 July 2008 at Holy Cross Church, Dundrum.

Chapter 2

First Steps to Government

LIKE THE LATE MARTIN LUTHER KING, Séamus "had a dream" and lived that dream through the many Government roles he filled during a long career at the forefront of Irish politics – not counting the years previously spent as backbench Deputy, Senator and General Secretary of Fianna Fáil. The Munster MEP, Brian Crowley, once said that "A man without dreams is like a golden winged eagle that cannot fly".

But the dream ended abruptly on 6 May 2008 when ill health forced Séamus Brennan to retire from Government at a time when he was perceived by many people – political commentators and some bookmakers – to be in line for the position of Tanaiste and/or Minister for Finance under Brian Cowen's first Government, with a real possibility of being appointed as the European Commissioner from Ireland when Charlie McCreevy had completed his term of office in Brussels. As a ten times minister, Séamus's unique record would certainly have put him in pole position for a senior European portfolio had events not ordained otherwise.

While there was a glimmer of light that the retirement would be temporary, it was probably more in hope than anything else. Cancer finally stole Séamus from his family in Dublin and Galway, and from his professional work colleagues, friends, constituents, political party and Irish public life generally, just two months later on 9 July 2008.

His career as a minister in Government had lasted from 10 March 1987 and it was as much a shock to those who worked with him day in and day out as it was to the many loyal constituents and Fianna Fáil members who equally felt the loss, along with his family and extended relations in Dublin, Galway and further afield.

But back in 1979, Séamus had been a Senator for the previous two years, and felt that he could no longer work as General Secretary following Jack Lynch's retirement and replacement by Charles Haughey. He resigned after serving for six years and began to think seriously about running for the Dáil himself over many strategy sessions with close friends such as Eoin O'Brien, Don Hall and Bob Manson Sr. Eventually, the decision was taken that he would definitely go for a Dáil seat and it seemed as if there were three possibilities: Galway, or a slice of George Colley's old constituency which had become available in Dublin North-East, or, since he lived in Dublin South, it was logical to consider that constituency as well.

Séamus promptly ruled out Galway, as he had been away from there for too long, and so the focus shifted to the Dublin North-East possibility. Don Hall was dubious and insisted that Séamus "take a look" at the constituency. He brought him to a little stream near Cadbury's factory in Coolock which formed part of the boundary between Dublin North-East and Dublin North-Central (Charlie Haughey's constituency). That sealed the possibility of Dublin North-East being in the reckoning as Séamus did not want to be that physically close to his old political adversary.

And so Dublin South was chosen and the campaign effectively began long before there was a general election. Séamus reckoned that "a good campaign" would win the day for him and he began to quietly recruit a team around him as there would not be enough time to do all that when an election was called.

The chance came in 1981 when a general election was called for June. He managed to get nominated by the constituency organisation in Dublin South and on being selected, found that he was running for the Dáil on a Fianna Fáil ticket which included two prominent outgoing Members of Dáil Éireann, Niall Andrews and Sile de Valera, along with an up and coming County Council-

lor called Tom Kitt. Fianna Fáil had added Sile to the newly created five seat Dublin South constituency after Andrews, Brennan
and Kitt had been selected at the convention, a move which was
interpreted at the time as an attempt by Charlie Haughey to prevent Séamus Brennan winning a seat. John Downing, in his 2004
political biography of Bertie Ahern, *Most Skilful, Most Devious,
Most Cunning*, was more direct: "Haughey had specifically can-
vassed against him (Brennan) and in favour of Sile de Valera."
Andrews and de Valera were both staunch supporters of Charlie
Haughey, in stark contrast to the former General Secretary of Fianna Fáil who was known to be strongly against the Haughey
leadership. De Valera's support for Haughey was particularly surprising given that records show that her grandfather, the former
President of Ireland and founder of Fianna Fáil, Eamon de Valera,
had completely distrusted Haughey and allegedly had told colleagues that Fianna Fáil would be destroyed if Haughey ever got
into a leadership role.

But former Taoiseach Jack Lynch, who still commanded a con-
siderable amount of support, came out of retirement to support
Séamus in his bid for the Dáil – and if Haughey's objective to keep
Brennan out was the plan, it spectacularly backfired.

The voters decided they wanted Séamus (some called him "a
new breath of fresh air") and elected him to the twenty-second
Dáil with 7,779 first preference votes compared to 5,690 for Andrews, 5,408 for de Valera, and 2,636 for Kitt. Séamus's first preference vote in the constituency was second only to the great Fine
Gael legend, John Kelly, who received 7,964 votes, but after transfers were counted, Séamus was actually the first TD to be elected.
He was followed by three Fine Gael TDs (John Kelly, Nuala
Fennell and Alan Shatter) and the sitting Fianna Fáil TD, Niall
Andrews, who had to content himself with being elected to the last
seat. Sile de Valera was not elected and after one more unsuccessful attempt at staying in Dublin South, she moved to the old constituency of her grandfather in Clare where she had better electoral success in later years. Tom Kitt would have to wait six more
years to be elected.

That election in Dublin South had been very hard fought by Fianna Fáil, not just with the other parties, but with Fianna Fáil members who had divided into separate groups for each of their three candidates. One of Séamus's favourite sayings was, "The most important thing in life is to have your own people", and that could very well have been the mantra for his electioneering as many members of Fianna Fáil Cumainn in the constituency did not welcome the arrival of this well known anti-Haugheyite, and they certainly did not go too far out of their way to canvass with him at that time. Séamus knew this was going to be the case and had been working for months to assemble around him a large group of solid canvassers, some of whom were in Fianna Fáil while many others did not have any particular political allegiance apart from wishing to support Séamus.

At the end, for Fianna Fáil to secure two of the five seats, and for Brennan to be in the lead on his first outing, was an astonishing feat given that before the constituency boundary was redrawn for that election, Fine Gael held three out of three seats in the old Dublin South County constituency. However, the Dublin South success was not repeated nationally for Fianna Fáil, and it was Fine Gael and Labour who formed the Government with Garret FitzGerald as Taoiseach and Michael O'Leary as Tanaiste.

But no sooner had he got his size eight shoes under the table in his Dáil office when Séamus was on the hustings again in less than eight months on 18 February 1982. The Fine Gael/Labour Coalition collapsed on a Budget provision which the Minister for Finance, John Bruton, wanted to bring in which would have imposed VAT on children's shoes. The Dublin South line-up for that election was the same as 1981 and resulted in all five outgoing TDs being returned. This time, it was Fianna Fáil in Government for the twenty-third Dáil with Charlie Haughey as Taoiseach and Ray MacSharry as Tanaiste. But it was to be a Government as short-lived as its predecessor.

Although a minority Government, it enjoyed the full support of Independent Deputy Tony Gregory, and the tacit support of other Independents and the Workers Party. The end came because Independents and the Workers Party withdrew support which resulted in the opposition winning a vote of no confidence in Mr. Haughey as Taoiseach. The motion for the vote, ironically, was tabled by Independent Fianna Fáil TD, Charlie McCreevy, who had been expelled from the Fianna Fáil Parliamentary Party in December 1981 after he gave a newspaper interview which strongly criticised Mr. Haughey.

The election that nobody wanted, being the third within 18 months, was held on 24 November 1982. While it was not the shortest Dáil in Irish history, there had never been three elections in such a short span of time. In Dublin South, with Sile de Valera gone to Clare, another historical name was on the ballot paper – Ruairi Brugha, son of the 1916 leader and former Minister for Defence, Cathal Brugha. Ruairi had run the famous Kingston's Shoe Shop in Dublin's O'Connell Street for many years, the street where, ironically, his father had been mortally wounded during the Civil War in 1922. While Ruairi had represented the old Dublin South County constituency with distinction for four years, and had been a Member of the European Parliament from 1977 to 1979 and a Senator, this was his first time to contest a general election in the new constituency. Running with him and Séamus were Niall Andrews and Tom Kitt. When the votes were counted, the outgoing TDs, Séamus and Niall Andrews, were returned to join the three outgoing Fine Gael TDs, John Kelly, Alan Shatter and Nuala Fennell. The twenty-fourth Dáil saw Garret FitzGerald as Taoiseach again, but this time with the new Labour Party Leader, Dick Spring, as Tanaiste.

After such a spate of elections, Séamus was now about to see some dramatic events unfold which would seriously distract both him and the country for years to come.

Charlie Haughey served as the sixth Taoiseach of Ireland from 1979 to 1981, March 1982 to December 1982 and from 1987 to 1992. He was a man with a colourful history – from marrying the Taoiseach's daughter (Maureen Lemass), to being a sacked Minister for Finance, to being charged with an alleged 1970 involvement in plans to smuggle guns to Northern Ireland during the height of what are known historically as "The Troubles", a charge for which he was acquitted following a trial. Then in 1982, the most wanted man in the country (the murderer Malcolm Macarthur) was found in the apartment of the Attorney General, Patrick Connolly, and the situation was described by Haughey at a subsequent press conference as "grotesque, unbelievable, bizarre and unprece- dented". The use of these adjectives was later to be concisely de- scribed by former Labour Minister, diplomat and writer, Conor Cruise O'Brien, by the acronym "GUBU".

Back in 1969, an Election year, the *Evening Herald* had a story that Haughey had sold his old home at Grangemore in Raheny to the Gallagher Group (who were prominent builders and develop- ers at that time) for something over £200,000 (€254,000). Ac- cording to the story, Haughey then acquired 250 acres in North Dublin (Abbeville in Kinsealy) for around £140,000 (€178,000). Not a bad deal at all, especially when he subsequently sold a small number of acres for around €10 million to settle a tax bill, and later again sold the remainder of the estate to Joe Moran of Manor Park Homes for some €45 million.

But it was the ongoing questions and rumours about how a public representative like Charlie Haughey could have accumu- lated his apparent wealth on a TD's and minister's salary that dog- ged the country, as later events in tribunals were also to do. At any rate, a number of Fianna Fáil TDs, including Séamus Brennan, wanted to test the mood and see if a more publicly acceptable per- son could be installed as leader of Fianna Fáil. The business prem- ises of Eoin O'Brien, 99 St. Stephen's Green, was a central meeting place for like-minded Oireachtas members such as Séamus Bren- nan, David Andrews, Des O'Malley, Liam Lawlor and Charlie McCreevy. Public relations guru Don Hall (son of RTÉ's Frank Hall) was also there as the strategies were pored over. On three dramatic occasions, attempts were made to replace Haughey. While all of them were ultimately unsuccessful, a significant level of minority support was evident.

The final heave in 1983 saw Des O'Malley challenge directly for the leadership of Fianna Fáil, and the resulting vote of 55 for

Haughey and 22 for O'Malley gave rise to what has become known in Fianna Fáil history as the "Gang of 22", and included Mary Harney, David Andrews, Bobby Molloy and Willie O'Dea among others. Séamus Brennan was firmly in that camp, though it caused him considerable personal stress that Fianna Fáil under Haughey had become so deeply divided. He resolved at that time to neither be involved in, nor to organise, any further attempts to dislodge Haughey, saying "let the hare sit", especially since key supporters would no longer be in the Fianna Fáil family. He believed time, or another day, would resolve the Haughey issue, but little did he know what would emerge about Haughey in later years as a result of allegations at tribunals set up by the Oireachtas.

The BBC Ireland (and former RTÉ) correspondent, Leo Enright, once said: "You know, I have a theory about Charlie Haughey. If you give him enough rope, he'll hang you." That certainly seemed to be the case as far as Séamus and other like-minded people were concerned, and he never expected to advance his national political role while Haughey was Fianna Fáil Leader and Taoiseach. Charlie appeared to have a Houdini-like trait which allowed him to escape just as it seemed all was doomed – though later history replicated the fact that even Houdini became a cropper in the end.

When there was talk of forming a new political party in the spring of 1985 by a number of Séamus's allies (including Des O'Malley, Mary Harney, David Andrews, Bobby Molloy, Pearse Wyse and Martin O'Donoghue), it was speculated that Séamus would leave Fianna Fáil. Among those who held this view was Cork businessman and concert promoter Barra O Tuama, who had discussions with Séamus and others, and later commissioned and paid for a poll by Irish Marketing Surveys to gauge the public reaction to a new political party headed by Des O'Malley. That poll showed 39 per cent in favour with 35 per cent against, a result which had mixed reviews. But for those intent on launching a new party, it proved to be decisive, particularly as it followed on the heels of another poll which showed that Des O'Malley's expulsion had caused a substantial drop in Fianna Fáil support.

On one famous occasion, Séamus was visiting the Rathgar home of Des O'Malley (who was a godfather to one of Séamus's daughters, as was Jack Lynch to another daughter). Also present were a number of other people who were opposed to Haughey. RTÉ had somehow got wind of this, put two and two together – but did not get four. Thinking there was a good story, they sent a reporter (Yvonne Murphy, who subsequently became a District Court Judge and husband of Supreme Court Judge, Adrian Hardiman) to check out the scene. As a media-friendly politician, Séamus was not going to pretend he was not there and came out to meet her with a glass in one hand and a savoury in the other, uttering the words which have gone into political legend, "Sure I'm only here on a social occasion visiting some friends".

In the autumn of 1985, a time which has become known as the turbulent 1980s due to economic downturn and strident debates on Ireland's future, the Progressive Democrats were founded. The impetus for this new party had stemmed from the dual expulsion of Des O'Malley from Fianna Fáil earlier that year for conduct unbecoming a member of Fianna Fáil when he refused to support Fianna Fáil's rejection of the introduction of contraception, and Mary Harney's expulsion over her support for the Anglo-Irish Agreement which had been brokered by the Fine Gael/Labour coalition. While neither of them had wanted to split the party, or to leave it, their fate was sealed by Haughey's personal crusade against them. According to Stephen Collins in his book, *Breaking the Mould*, Des O'Malley declared to his co-founders that it was "crucial to have a good General Secretary and that he wanted to find a Séamus Brennan type". It was a mark of Séamus's political and administrative skills that Des O'Malley would use Séamus as a template for the person he wanted.

Séamus had been very active in discussing the possibilities for a new party, and when a favourable view came from the poll results the expectation of Séamus getting involved became stronger – but that was never an option despite conflicting advice from some of Séamus's family and acquaintances. Mary Harney was one who agreed that Séamus was unlikely to leave Fianna Fáil. He was born into Fianna Fáil and was not prepared to abandon the ship just because he did not like the captain, although he also accepted that it was futile to continue opposing the Haughey leadership.

In the early days of 1986, Séamus felt that he had to try to persuade wavering Fianna Fáil TDs to stay with Fianna Fáil. When the Cork TD, Pearse Wyse, was prominently speculated as being a recruit for the new party, Séamus and Bobby Molloy went to him but did not get any assurances of his loyalty to Fianna Fáil, and sure enough, Pearse Wyse appeared at a Progressive Democrat rally in Cork soon after.

But three days later, an even more remarkable event took place – Bobby Molloy turned up at a Progressive Democrat rally in Galway and sealed his own departure from Fianna Fáil.

Although some former Fianna Fáil people still harboured the hope that Séamus would join up with them in the Progressive Democrats, he remained true to his original political roots, all the while retaining the same degree of friendship with his former parliamentary colleagues that existed previously.

Back in 1985, the dual mandate was still in place, where a County Councillor could also be a TD or Senator. In the local elections that year, Fianna Fáil desperately needed a household name to run in the Rathfarnham Electoral Area of the old Dublin County Council with the sitting Councillor, Ann Ormonde, who subsequently went on to be elected as a Senator and ran for the Dáil on a number of occasions along with Séamus. The household name required was Séamus Brennan, and significant political pressure was brought to bear on Séamus, as an Opposition backbench TD, to let his name go forward. While he was reluctant, he was dutiful as always to his party, accepted the challenge, went forward at the convention and was selected. As expected, he duly won the seat (along with Ann Ormonde) and thereby found himself in the unique position of having been elected to the Dáil before he was a County Councillor. As he said, tongue in cheek, after his election: "I always wanted to be a County Councillor!" But in truth he had no burning ambition to ever be a County Councillor. He had gone through significant political hoops over the years since becoming professionally involved in politics and had only run for the Council because the party needed his name to be on the ballot paper.

In 1981 and 1982, after the first three general elections of his career, Séamus had been asked to co-author *Nealon's Guide to Dáil and Seanad* in conjunction with Fine Gael TD, Minister of State and former RTÉ current affairs broadcaster, Ted Nealon. The Guide had been produced since 1973 under just Ted Nealon's name but it was felt that it needed a comparable political name for the future who could mirror the analytical skills of the legendary Ted Nealon. Séamus was well known as a comparable political analyst and was in his element with this opportunity to add an important new string to his bow. Having had a taste for being an author, he followed it up in February 1986 with his own *Brennan's Key to Local Authorities*, which was described as "the first ever comprehensive publication on Local Authority Elections". This was produced in conjunction with his friend Eric Murphy, with assistance from a number of people including the author of this book. *Brennan's Key* was for Local Authorities what the *Nealon's Guide* was for Dáil and Seanad, namely an invaluable reference book for politicians, journalists, business people, political activists and, as the introduction to his book said, "anyone interested in Irish elections and the personalities involved".

But he did not continue that book for succeeding local elections, nor did he co-author any further issues of *Nealon's Guide* as he wanted to concentrate on what was to become the first rung in his unique ministerial career.

He served as a County Councillor for two years when, much to his relief, Fianna Fáil won the 1987 general election, thus ending four years of Fine Gael and Labour in Government under Garret FitzGerald and Dick Spring. He was replaced on the County Council by Stephen Riney, who had been the unsuccessful Fianna Fáil candidate in Rathfarnham in 1985.

The general election to the twenty-fifth Dáil on 17 February 1987 saw Séamus's vote significantly exceed that of the long-serving John Kelly (9,940 first preferences for Séamus and 7,247 for Kelly). Kelly was joined by Alan Shatter (5,720 votes) and together they took the two last seats, which was a major turnaround for what had been considered a Fine Gael area. That election also saw Tom Kitt elected for the first time with 8,423 first preference votes. However, the poll topper in Dublin South was Anne Colley (the first outing for the two-years-old Progressive Democrats winning 14 seats nationally) with 11,957 votes, a feat which would be dramatically reduced in the following election in 1989.

Anne Colley was herself a granddaughter of a former Fianna Fáil TD, Henry Colley, and one of four daughters and three sons of former Fianna Fáil Tanaiste, George Colley. George was arguably the most strident arch-enemy of Charlie Haughey and, as a result, had a natural affinity with Séamus. A former Fine Gael Minister, Gemma Hussey, writing in her cabinet diaries, recorded how "upset" Séamus had been when Colley's body was brought back from London, where he had died on 17 September 1983. Colley had been viewed by many as an alternative Fianna Fáil leader having challenged for the leadership in 1966 (against Jack Lynch) and in 1979 (against Haughey). In that first leadership challenge, Haughey and Neil Blaney were also candidates, but they withdrew when Jack Lynch threw his hat in the ring leaving the fight to succeed Sean Lemass between Colley and Lynch, even though Haughey, as Lemass's son-in-law, had hoped to capitalise on his relationship with the outgoing Taoiseach. Lynch won easily by 59 votes to 19. However, it was the latter election that really galvanised political interest after the long wait for what was seen as the battle of the decade: Colley v. Haughey.

As George Colley had the support of most of the cabinet, it was expected that this perceived influence would help wavering backbenchers on whom Haughey relied on for support. The tight result (38 for Colley and 44 for Haughey) marked a distinct turning point for Fianna Fáil, but the closeness of it was also responsible for Colley being able to remain as Tanaiste in Haughey's first Government and being able to demand a veto on the appointment of the Minister for Justice and the Minister for Defence. Colley felt the veto power was necessary because of the particular sensitivity of these two posts due to the arms trial events of 1970, despite Haughey's subsequent acquittal of all charges. The history of Ireland and of Fianna Fáil would have been very different if George Colley had won the leadership that time.

A minority Fianna Fáil Government was formed on 10 March 1987 with the support of Independent Tony Gregory, and the qualified support of Fine Gael in what was known as the "Tallaght Strategy" under their new leader, Alan Dukes. This was a major departure for Fine Gael, and subsequently for Alan Dukes himself, who had gambled that supporting the Government in the national interest at a time of financial difficulty was more important than party politics, as long as the Government adopted Fine Gael economic policies. In the end, Dukes received little credit, being replaced as party leader by the end of the decade, while Fine Gael was rewarded with an increase of only four seats in the following general election. History may be kinder to Dukes as it is still seen by many people as being the right thing to do at the time.

Thus, Charlie Haughey was elected Taoiseach for the second time with Brian Lenihan Sr. as Tanaiste. With Haughey again in power, Séamus was firmly expecting to spend some more years on the backbenches. One rationale for that view was concisely put by author and political journalist John Cooney, writing in the *Western People*, when he said that as a political correspondent in the 1980s, he "often heard unprintable descriptions from the vitriolic tongue of either Haughey himself or his closest henchmen expressing their loathing and distrust of Brennan". Séamus himself was aware of the feelings and he was not hopeful of ever achieving ministerial office under Haughey.

But despite the difficult history between them, Mr. Haughey to his credit displayed the vision which characterised the many good things he did for Ireland. In this case, it seems that he recognised and prized talent and electoral success so much that he was able to put them above personal animosity. It would appear that he understood the actions of the previous years were motivated by robust political differences and were not purely personal. Equally,

Séamus was also prepared to bite his lip and see what he could do for the country.

And so Séamus became the first ever Minister for Trade and Marketing at the Department of Industry and Commerce based in Kildare Street – the first time in the history of the State that the importance of marketing as an aspect of wealth creation was adequately recognised by devoting an office of Government to it. Thus began his ministerial career just short of six years after entering Dáil Éireann on a significant first rung of what one former British Prime Minister, Benjamin Disraeli, called "the greasy pole", a quotation which was also used in a 1981 episode of the BBC comedy series, *Yes Minister*. Although the post was as a junior minister, Séamus was designated as a "super junior" which gave him the right to attend cabinet meetings. The senior minister was Albert Reynolds who would go on to become Taoiseach and fifth leader of Fianna Fáil in 1992.

That first period in Government very soon had commentators recognising the new kid on the ministerial block. Séamus had already become a well known political star performer on television and radio through his regular outings as Fianna Fáil General Secretary and backbench TD, and as a result became the most high profile of the junior ministers at the time. His natural flair for broadcasting put him well ahead of his Leinster House peers in more senior positions, and probably contributed greatly to the success of Carr Communications (run by Bunny Carr, Terry Prone and Tom Savage) where many of his political peers went, or were sent, for media training. Media exposure is one thing, but Séamus always believed in having substance behind such exposure. "A politician will very quickly be found out if their only ability is an ability to perform for the media," was a favourite saying of his to up and coming public representatives when he was giving one of his regular briefings arranged by Fianna Fáil headquarters to activate aspiring and new politicians.

And so he began to throw himself into his brief and to absorb the complexities of having responsibility for selling Ireland and of being one of the chief supporters of business in the Government.

Having had a background in business through his father being a builder, and with commerce degrees from University College Galway and University College Dublin, he was well placed to be a strong and vigorous advocate for business in Government. He had dreamt of this opportunity for many years and was now going to give it everything he had.

His immediate staff were Ciaran O Cuinneagain (Private Secretary); Ray Kinsella (Economic Adviser) who was recruited from his role as an economist with the Central Bank; this author (Political Adviser), recruited from his position as General Manager of a marketing company); and Mary Browne, who was his Oireachtas secretary when he was a Senator and previously had worked with John Bruton when he was Parliamentary Secretary to the Minister for Education, 1973–1977. The latter two would remain with Séamus throughout his ministerial career.

As the first Minister for Marketing, he was singled out by being made an Honorary Member of the Marketing Institute of Ireland, a recognition that he personally valued very highly, particularly as the former Taoiseach, Sean Lemass, had been President of the Institute for a number of years after his retirement.

Just a few months into his ministry, Séamus was in the throes of complex legislation called the Export Promotion (Amendment) Bill 1987, which publicly tested the span of his thinking and animated the export sector. The Bill dealt with Special Trading Houses, modelled on a Japanese system but ahead of their time in Western Europe, which would offer Irish companies the export marketing skills they could not acquire for themselves. He wanted to provide what he called "a toolbox for exporters" to help focus the national export effort on those areas where the best results could be delivered in the shortest possible time. With this legislation, he had successfully demonstrated his capacity to absorb the minutiae of a Government Bill and the ability to engage with people who had enjoyed the fruits of marketing international brands. This was a further string to his bow and marked him higher on the scale of forward thinkers – and a person to watch for the future.

Speaking on the Bill in the Oireachtas in July 1987, Séamus gave what were then very frank comments for a Government Minister:

> Our biggest industrial weakness is in international marketing but while we have recognised the disease, we have done precious little up to now to bring about a cure.

His aim was to provide a framework which would utilise the:

> ... people and companies with special knowledge of certain markets or who possess certain language skills that are in rare supply. Some companies have exportable products but do not have any resources. On the other hand, we have to recognise that there is now in Ireland a considerable reservoir of export marketing experience that we can put to more effective use.

This was to be done by licensing companies, Special Trading Houses, whose sole business was the sale abroad of a variety of Irish goods which were not manufactured by them and which were only sold to the overseas wholesale market. Effectively, it was like an updated co-operative which would allow someone with special knowledge of a particular product area, or of a particular geographical market, to set up a specialist company with the sole purpose of exporting Irish goods into that market.

Being acutely conscious of the need to avoid any unnecessary administrative burdens on business, Séamus put it on the record that:

> ... my objective is not to put an obstacle in the way of enterprise but merely to put up a fence to keep the cowboys out. We cannot, and indeed should not, do the job of these companies for them. No State should be in the business of mollycoddling private companies who are not prepared to make an effort for themselves. What this State should be in is the business of helping companies

to overcome the handicaps they suffer through being, for the most part, small enterprises in a small economy.

But his career in Government nearly ended prematurely.

On a car journey from Clifden (where he was on holiday in the summer of 1987) to Galway for a radio interview (these were the days before mobile phones were widely available), his official car skidded, crashed into a wall near Oughterard, and was a total write off. The accident left Séamus in hospital in Galway, but miraculously he suffered only bruising from his seat belt and was discharged within days. However, his official driver, Joe Callinan, was unconscious after the accident and remained in hospital for substantially longer. Thankfully, both recovered from that traumatic incident and its aftermath.

Back in the office and in fighting form, Séamus began the task of asking 15 business-minded people if they would serve the country as members of a new national marketing group, and having succeeded in getting their approval, he set it up on 20 January 1988 (see Appendix 2 for full list of membership).

In answer to a Dáil question from John Bruton a year later on 1 February 1989, Séamus said that the role of this group was "to advise the Government on practical measures to boost the marketing performance of Irish firms on export and home markets". He added that the group "had met on eight occasions to date, including an all-day session at Barrettstown" and had "formulated a number of proposals for inclusion in a National Marketing Plan". Also at Séamus's side at this time was Eoin O'Brien, who ran the English Language Studies Institute, and as a commercial educationalist had a particular interest in overseas marketing.

After about 18 months or so, the Economic Adviser, Ray Kinsella, decided to move on and took up a post as a professor at the University of Ulster in Coleraine, and later at the Smurfit Graduate School of Business in UCD. He was replaced by Dick Doyle, an IDA executive, who had initially been reluctant to leave the IDA, but was persuaded by his then boss, IDA Chief Padraic White (husband of Mary White, co-founder of Lir Chocolates who went on to become a Fianna Fáil Senator), to give it a whirl. Little did he know that three months after coming on board, an unexpected general election would be held which would result in the first ever Coalition Government involving Fianna Fáil.

As a result, the torch for the marketing of Ireland into the future and the National Marketing Plan was to be left to new incoming Minister for Trade and Marketing, Terry Leyden, who would take up where Séamus had left off.

Chapter 3

Upwards to Cabinet

THE GENERAL ELECTION FOR THE twenty-sixth Dáil on 15 June 1989 came about quite suddenly, and in fact was widely thought to be unnecessary. While the minority Fianna Fáil Government had suffered a defeat in the Dáil on a motion about funding for those suffering from AIDS, it alone was not a reason for dissolving the Dáil. The real reason had more to do with opinion polls which indicated that an overall majority was possible and Charlie Haughey decided to take a gamble on the basis that the opposition would not be ready to mount a strong campaign – but on this, Haughey had made a crucial tactical mistake which would cost him dearly.

Throughout the snap election campaign, for which Charlie Haughey had appointed Séamus as National Director of Elections, there was no obvious talk of Fianna Fáil abandoning its belief in single party Government – and for historical reasons, it was not an easy belief to jettison. However, there were those in the party who had a view that all options should be kept open and all lines of communication developed because you never know what result an election will turn up – and, as it subsequently turned out, they were quite right.

The election resulted in a double personal triumph for Séamus – the party retaining Government and he topping the poll, not just in Dublin South but in the entire country, with 13,927 first preference votes, while Tom Kitt was second on 7,217. Previous poll topper, Anne Colley, secured only 4,607 votes compared to the 11,957 she received just two years earlier and was not re-elected. The outgoing Fine Gael TD, John Kelly, had retired and his place was taken by Nuala Fennell (4,983 votes) who joined outgoing Fine Gael TD, Alan Shatter (7,969 votes) That election also saw the first ever Green Party TD elected when, even to his own amazement, Roger Garland secured 4,771 first preference votes. After some transfers, he had beaten Nuala Fennell to take the fourth seat. But Colley was not the only setback for the Progressive Democrats – eight of their 14 seats were lost nationally.

However, as things turned out, the remaining six seats for the Progressive Democrats combined with Fianna Fáil's 77 seats gave the bare majority needed for Government. The problem was that Fianna Fáil had never shared power before, though it was quickly realised that the national interest required Fianna Fáil to give up its one-party Government policy. Negotiations were begun and Séamus was asked to play a leading role in view of his close friendships with most of the Progressive Democrat TDs.

After a month of negotiating, the first Fianna Fáil/Progressive Democrat Coalition Government took office on 12 July 1989. And once again, despite their historic personal differences, Mr. Haughey clearly recognised and valued the work which Séamus did as a junior minister (and in helping to negotiate the historic pact with the Progressive Democrats) as he appointed him to the senior post of Minister for Tourism and Transport (with Communications added a year later after those responsibilities were moved from the Minister for Justice, Ray Burke). His personal staff of Dick Doyle, this author and Mary Browne moved with him to the ground floor of the same building in Kildare Street where he had served as Minister for Trade and Marketing for the previous two years. His new Private Secretary was Dominick McBride.

This portfolio suited Séamus immensely, quite apart from his sheer delight at being appointed to a senior post in cabinet – it was the fulfilment of another part of his cherished dream to serve the country as a senior minister. His background in Galway was partially steeped in tourism through the small guest house run by his mother, and this complemented the business experience of his

father being a self-employed builder and his own commercial
training.

On his very first day, before he even had sight of his new office
in the department, it happened that Aer Lingus was to take delivery of a new generation of airliner and Séamus made his own arrangements to be on hand at Dublin Airport for its arrival, which
surprised the staff in his new department as they were used to
making any arrangements for their minister, particularly when it
involved semi-state bodies. But Séamus wanted to establish his
own independence of action, and initiated a direct contact with
Aer Lingus and with Aer Rianta, which at that time was the airport
operating authority. He was his own man and while he would always listen to and respect the advice given by his department officials, the final decision would be his own at all times. This was to
be a significant barometer in his dealings with all subsequent departments. Officials in each department quickly found out that
Séamus was definitely a new broom and they had to adjust to the
"pocket dynamo" (as Séamus was described by Jim McGuire in the
Western People on another occasion) coming among them.

He came to this ministry in an era of high airline fares where
only the very lucky could ever afford to go abroad for holidays.
Step into the breach the "pocket dynamo" who wanted to make air
travel affordable for more Irish people, as he strongly believed
that tourists from Ireland would simultaneously be ambassadors
for Ireland when abroad.

The fledgling airline Ryanair (named after its founders, the
family of Tony Ryan) had begun operations in 1985 with share
capital of IR£1 (€1.27), a staff of 25, one 15-seater turbo-prop aircraft and a route from Waterford to London Gatwick. Five months
after the first flights from Waterford, Ryanair applied for and was
granted a licence to fly between Dublin and Luton, which provided
its entry into direct competition with Aer Lingus, and two old Vis-
count aircraft were sourced for the route. The ultimate goal was to
do in Western Europe what Southwest Airlines had done in the
US, and what Freddie Laker tried to do between 1977 and 1982
with his Skytrain on transatlantic routes – namely, to have cheap,

no frills travel. The problem was that Aer Lingus, the State airline, had an effective monopoly (along with British Airways) on high capacity routes between Ireland and Britain. Many hours of battle between the two airlines led to Ryanair making a complaint to the European Commission concerning the alleged abuse of a dominant position by Aer Lingus under EU competition rules. Coincidentally, Freddie Laker had taken a similar case to law and a US court later ruled that some 29 established airlines had been using illegal price pressure to put Laker out of business. However, unlike Freddie Laker, Ryanair is still going strong after 24 years.

In February 1989, Dr. Sean Barrett, a well respected transport economist at Trinity College, had estimated that Ryanair's impact on fares, time savings and increased British visitors was responsible for a gain of over IR£200 million (€254 million) in revenue for the Irish economy. However, the airline had reported losses in 1988 of over IR£7.5 million (€9.5 million), and its board, with Chief Executive P.J. McGoldrick, was on the brink of recommending the closure of the airline with the loss of over 500 jobs in Ireland, together with the associated spin-offs at airports and in the tourism industry, unless there was a further substantial capital investment from its shareholders. According to McGoldrick, the management of the airline was "unable to recommend" that the shareholders inject more money unless the anti-competitive situation was changed. However, should that change come about, the shareholders had undertaken to provide up to IR£20 million (€25.4 million) to address accumulated losses and to create what McGoldrick called "other tourism and leisure-related investments in Ireland".

When the complaint to the EU Commission was duly investigated, it was found to have sufficient grounds to warrant attention, much to the relief of Ryanair. With so much at stake, the Government had to take early action. There was a view being expressed (mainly by Ryanair) that the Department of Transport was the downtown office of Aer Lingus, and there was some truth in that. Whenever airline policy needed a view or an analysis, the department would normally ask Aer Lingus for their comments.

Invariably, Aer Lingus would be negative if a proposal had the potential to impact on their own services, and clearly any proposal for Ryanair to cut into their market was not going to get their blessing. The use of Aer Lingus in that way had to change. Also, the huge increase in air travellers between Ireland and Britain (doubling from 1.5 million in four years) could no longer be ignored. Monopolies were anathema to Séamus Brennan as he believed they were bad for the consumer and he ordered an immediate review of the recent performance of the two Irish airlines and of Government airline policy generally. He recognised that there was a contradiction in the State being the owner of an airline while also being the regulator: "You can't be a referee and play on one of the teams at the same time."

On 20 September 1989, Séamus announced a new policy which he had advocated and steered through the Government. He said the policy "will be to focus aviation policy on a strengthening of the Irish presence rather than having two Irish carriers actively pursuing traffic on identical routes".

The new two-airline policy was to be rolled out immediately as follows:

- London – allow Aer Lingus exclusivity on Heathrow and Gatwick (96 per cent of London traffic); allow Ryanair exclusivity on Stanstead (a new and then remote airport) and Luton (4 per cent of London traffic).

- Paris – Aer Lingus to be the sole Irish carrier

- Munich – Ryanair to be the sole Irish carrier

- Liverpool – Ryanair to be the sole Irish carrier.

- Manchester – Aer Lingus to be the sole Irish carrier.

- Regional airports – Ryanair to be the sole Irish carrier providing direct services from Irish regional airports and the UK/Continental Europe; Aer Lingus to continue serving these routes via their Dublin hub.

- New Routes – Where an Irish carrier develops international air services on a new route, another Irish carrier will not be allowed on the route during the development phase which was set at two years.

This had all been achieved without any financial help from the State for Ryanair, which would have been difficult anyway given that the State had a responsibility for Aer Lingus. But it gave Ryanair the opportunity to prove itself while also protecting Aer Lingus — the best of both worlds. It was probably also a remarkable achievement given that the Taoiseach, Charlie Haughey, and the Minister for Labour, Bertie Ahern, both represented north Dublin constituencies which were home to thousands of Aer Lingus and Dublin Airport employees — potential votes to be lost for both of them. This new policy would really shake up any complacency that existed and open an important new door for the consumer. But that was the goal that Séamus had set and the Government had accepted. On more than one occasion, he had to remind people that he was Minister for Transport, not Minister for Aer Lingus, and his job was to develop the aviation industry for the benefit of the country as a whole.

It was not unexpected when the decision caused local mayhem among airline and airport employees, who felt that taking Aer Lingus away from some routes and giving Ryanair access would disturb the comfortable lives they had with Aer Lingus being dominant and effectively able to call the shots with Government. Union antagonism was brought sharply home when Séamus's home and constituency office were picketed by aviation employees brandishing banners which suggested that he was beholden to Ryanair. But he made it very clear that he had "no connection in any way" with Ryanair and had promoted the two-airline policy in the national interest, taking the view that two airlines would mean more people travelling. In fact, he would have been happy to see any number of other airlines opening up the market, whether they were Irish or otherwise, but Ryanair were the only ones to step up to the plate at the time.

The two-airline policy has been proven over the years to have been the bulwark of a successful plan, and it is somewhat ironic that today Aer Lingus often beats Ryanair on fares, while Ryanair has surpassed Aer Lingus in fleet size and passenger numbers. Both airlines continue to adjust their operations in the face of strongly negative pressures on aviation throughout the world and Irish consumers are the lucky beneficiaries.

But it was while giving an arranged interview on the RTÉ programme *Morning Ireland* that brought Séamus into the full glare of adverse media commentary without evidential backup. On the live programme, Séamus was repeatedly asked by the presenter, Cathal MacCoille, if Ryanair had secured what he called "these concessions" because of a financial contribution to Fianna Fáil. This line of questioning greatly annoyed and disturbed Séamus and he said on air that it was "most unfair". Later that day, the Government Press Secretary, P.J. Mara, made a formal complaint to RTÉ which led to the Director-General, Vincent Finn, issuing a written apology. However, this letter was not considered to be satisfactory and some days later, the Director-General went on air himself on *Morning Ireland* and said:

> I very much regret that such a question was put to you which carried an implication for which no evidence was provided. The implication was that you, as Minister, could be influenced in any decision by anything other than the relevant issues – an implication for which no evidence was provided.

With this broadcast apology, Séamus considered the matter to be closed but it did bring to his mind two quotations: "It takes 20 years to build a reputation and just five minutes to ruin it" (Warren Buffet, American entrepreneur) and "Glass, china and reputation are easily cracked, and never well mended" (Benjamin Franklin, American inventor and statesman).

But it was other unsupported comments that would be much more serious years later during his second tenure as Minister for Transport.

Another aviation progression under Séamus's leadership was the establishment of the Irish Aviation Authority as a commercial semi-state body. Up to this, it had been a division of the Department of Transport but the development of a growing aviation industry gave the impetus for making it a financially self-sufficient body which would also generate a significant dividend flow to the exchequer without the taxpayer having to pay for capital and current costs.

Flushed with the success of the new aviation policy, Séamus wanted to do something similar with Córas Iompar Éireann (CIÉ) which had a virtual monopoly on public transport. He focussed on a growing public demand for late night buses in the run up to Christmas 1989 – this was a time when there were not enough taxis in Dublin – and asked CIÉ to consider providing the services. The CIÉ unions shot down the suggestion and while trade union opposition would probably have been the death knell for others, Séamus was not a person to take "no" for an answer – as people were beginning to find out. The only option was to licence private operators on certain routes and so late night bus services were provided in Dublin for the first time. Later on, CIÉ saw how successful and profitable the business could be and came on board with proposals for other routes. It is now a normal part of public transport in Dublin each Christmas.

Séamus's zeal for reform was now firmly in the open for everyone to see. But he was also acutely conscious of the barriers that would be put in his way. While he was never accused of being Machiavellian, he said to me that his thoughts did turn to a saying from that Italian master of politics:

> It must be considered that there is nothing more difficult to carry out, nor more doubtful of success, nor more dangerous to handle, than to initiate a new order of things. For the reformer has enemies in all those who profit by the old order.

How true this was to be in his future ministries as he endeavoured to do what he thought was right for Ireland.

Another issue in CIÉ which annoyed Séamus was their accounting use of the considerable State subsidy as income so that their accounts always showed a profit. He believed this was disingenuous and ordered that future accounts should show the State subsidy as non-income coming in after normal income and expenses. This provided a much more transparent system for judging the use of taxpayer's funds and allowed everyone to see exactly what public transport was costing the taxpayer.

However, the local political significance of being Transport Minister became more apparent when it was recalled that as a Senator in 1985 Séamus had personally commissioned and paid for a professional study of the possibilities for the old Harcourt Street Railway Line. This old line had remained dormant (but largely in public ownership) since being closed down by the then Chairman of CIÉ, Todd Andrews, in the late 1950s. Niall Andrews (son of Todd) was a Fianna Fáil Member of the European Parliament since 1984 and a former Dáil colleague of Séamus's in Dublin South. It has been said that Niall did not wish to see any public transport use on the old Harcourt Street Railway as he felt it would reflect badly on his late father, who was also one of the founders of Fianna Fáil.

But needs must and Séamus persevered with the issue. He wanted to update the earlier study which showed that for a very small investment the route of the old railway could be used for a public transport corridor. One of his first acts was to set up a Departmental committee under Assistant Secretary John Lumsden to explore the issue. To ensure that the political implications were taken account of, given that a substantial chunk of the old line was in his own political heartland, he appointed this author, his Political Adviser, to be a member of the committee.

Going assiduously about the task, the committee gathered intelligence from a variety of sources including new systems at Essen in Germany and at Runcorn in England, where state-of-the-art guided busways had recently been opened. It was decided to visit both of these operations, but on the day of the Essen trip other urgent Government business caused it to be cancelled. Later on, the committee decided that there should be one field trip to complement the intelligence gathering and the facility at Runcorn was chosen. Arrangements were duly made, but in the end Séamus was again unable to travel. However, it was agreed that the trip should still take place and several of the committee members made an overnight return journey by road and sea using a small Imp bus which had been procured from Dublin Bus for the purpose. It was a sight to behold for British midlands residents to see a small vehicle with Dublin Bus livery travelling through their locality!

The success of that trip, combined with other information, proved again that the old Harcourt Street Line could be returned to public transport use at a relatively small cost. Outline plans were made in order to begin the process of making a strong case to secure the necessary funding from the Minister for Finance, Albert Reynolds. Séamus's powers of persuasion were already legendary and really came into their own at this time when it was revealed that the Minister for Finance agreed that a sum of £6 million (€7.6 million) would be provided for rebuilding several bridges between the Grand Canal and Leopardstown. Séamus was on his way to achieving a long-held dream – but it would be the middle of the next decade before the final realisation of his dream became reality.

The Minister for Justice in 1991, Ray Burke, had also held responsibility for Communications and had just completed the passage of his Radio and Television Act in the Oireachtas which allowed an Independent Broadcasting Commission to regulate the airwaves. This Act ended years of pirate radio and began a new era of independent commercial broadcasting, but questions were to be asked in later years about the relationship of Burke with those who wanted to get in on the ground floor of commercial broadcasting.

As the Act was now law, it was seen as a good time to disengage Communications from the Justice portfolio and it was transferred to Séamus. The broadening of his duties with the inclusion of Communications earned Séamus the nickname of "the Minister for Everything" because it seemed that he was almost a one-person Government being responsible for air, land and sea transport, along with his new responsibilities for everything on the airwaves.

It was also a good time to be Tourism Minister as substantial EU Structural Funds were available to develop the tourism product with hotels and golf courses being the significant beneficiaries. The foundation laid at that time hugely increased the availability of high quality hotel facilities and attendant leisure activities which proved to be a big tourist draw in subsequent years.

But it would be wrong to assume that everything was rosy in the garden.

B&I Line, the State-owned shipping company, was in serious difficulty with mounting debts and no capital to invest in the business. It was questionable why the State should still be involved in shipping at all, but historical reasons abounded going back to the days before mass airline transport was affordable.

The origin of the British & Irish Steam Packet Company goes back to 1836 when a number of Dublin businessmen got together in the Commercial Building in Dame Street and decided to bankroll a new shipping venture. Their first ships were three wooden paddle steamers. In 1965, the Minister for Transport, Erskine Childers (who later went on to become the fourth President of Ireland), on behalf of the Government took over the company along with 10 passenger and cargo vessels in order to secure the sea services for passenger and container traffic that was so essential for what was then a largely agricultural island economy.

In 1990, after successive loss-making years, Séamus sought Government approval to privatise the company as it was no longer necessary for the State to be involved in shipping when there was now mass competition available in both shipping and air. The tender process resulted in bids from Irish Continental Group/Irish Ferries, P + O, and Maersk which underlined the good sense in taking the decision to sell the B & I Line.

On 1 January 1992, Irish Continental Group/Irish Ferries took over the company for the nominal sum of IR£1 (€0.78) – the sting in the tail being that debts of some IR£90 million (€114.3 million) would also be taken on board.

A year before, Séamus had led tributes following the death of former Fine Gael TD John Kelly with whom he shared his Dublin

South constituency for many years. Although political opposites, they had many similarities in that both were extremely courteous, both were fully fluent in Irish, both had a great wit and both had tremendous clarity of thought. The main difference between them was their constituency work. It was often said that John Kelly would not entertain a constituent calling at his house in the affluent Ailesbury Road, whereas Séamus thrived on one-to-one contact with any constituent, be they millionaire or pauper. In a different world, or without the split of the Civil War in 1922–1923, a war which spawned Fianna Fáil and Fine Gael from the same historical origin, they might both have been of the same political persuasion for the closing years of the twentieth century.

Chapter 4

Time for Education

O N 11 FEBRUARY 1992, CHARLIE HAUGHEY resigned as Taoiseach and Albert Reynolds was elected in his place after Bertie Ahern withdrew. Some would say that Bertie ruled himself out
after snide questions were raised by opponents about where he
slept at night, while others believe that a secret deal was done
whereby Albert would nominate Bertie as the heir apparent.

In any event, Albert's first job as Taoiseach was to exercise his
Constitutional prerogative to reshuffle the Government and while
eight ministers were sacked, Séamus was retained but transferred
to another senior ministry in Education. In Albert Reynolds' un-
authorised biography by Tim Ryan (published in 1994), it was
suggested that Séamus had told Reynolds that he felt "Education
was wrong" for him, but on being reminded that Eamon de Valera
and Jack Lynch had both held the position, Séamus accepted the
transfer. But his time at the Department of Education was to be
short-lived.

His successor as Transport Minister was the current Taoiseach, Brian Cowen. Being from the midlands, Mr. Cowen did not
have the same attachment or affinity with prioritising the re-
opening of the Harcourt Street Line and the plan was mothballed,
though it would resurface in a dramatic way over the following
years.

Séamus arrived in Education after Mary O'Rourke had spent a
number of years in that department as minister. His new interim
Private Secretary was Frank Wyse, succeeded by Dermot Curran.
The pressing issue for the department was a commitment in the

"Programme for Economic and Social Progress" to produce a Green Paper (discussion document) on the future of education policy. While some preparatory work had been done by the previous minister, Séamus came in with a new broom and incorporated innovative thinking into the vocabulary of the department, particularly in the area of enterprise which he believed should be built-in to the school curriculum.

Just before the three traditional teacher conferences at Easter, his plans were advanced enough to produce an introduction document which he wanted the conferences to consider, given the crucial role of teachers in the system. This was to be part of his final Green Paper which would be out for full consultation before a White Paper (formal proposal) was produced. However, the teacher unions appeared to be less than pleased to have the document upsetting what Jim Higgins (Fine Gael) described in the Dáil as "the already tightly scheduled and pre-determined agenda of these organisations".

This was the sort of inflexibility which really annoyed Séamus. He had issued the document in good faith specifically to generate comments and opinions from teachers who were on the frontline of education, and what better place to do so than at their annual conferences at a time when they would not be preoccupied with their teaching duties. But it seemed that some people wanted to have their cake and eat it – he wondered to his political staff if teachers unions expected to have special paid time off from teaching to consider their views, rather than getting down to it at the conferences which he felt were always rather dull affairs designed more to satisfy the egos of union leaders than indulging in real debate. After all, it was not something which came out of the blue, having been well signalled by both Séamus and his predecessor, Mary O'Rourke, and as people knew by now, Séamus was not one to sit around while others attempted to stifle movement. He did not believe in the attraction of comfort and ease which power holders seemed to use to gain followers and to perpetuate their control over people – this was his lasting view of teachers unions, and given his experience with other unions in other portfolios it is hardly surprising that it coloured his view of trade union activity into the future.

As Minister for Education, he made a point of visiting schools at least once a week, and particularly liked the opportunity to speak to the senior secondary classes whenever he could. In those talks, he always stressed that an individual "can make a difference" in the world of politics. The phrase "You can make the difference" was later adopted by the European Parliament on some of its promotional material. Séamus's purpose was to energise and encourage students to look to involvement in politics when they left school. He had developed that line of thought from the words of author Rebecca Barlow Jordan:

> It's not how much you accomplish in life that really counts, but how much you give to others.
>
> It's not how high you build your dream that makes a difference, but how high your faith can climb.
>
> It's not how many goals you reach, but how many lives you touch.
>
> It's not who you know that matters, but who you are inside.
>
> Believe in the impossible, hold tight to the incredible, and live each day to its fullest potential.
>
> You can make a difference in your world.

As a fluent Irish speaker who had studied for his degrees through Irish at University College Galway, Séamus was always going to have considerable interest in the future of the language. During a debate on the RTÉ programme *Questions and Answers*, Séamus was up front in his comments:

> We are down to the wire on the Irish language. Either we take it really seriously or we give up on it – and I don't favour the latter course. One of the things I want to do in Education is to give more marks for speaking the language instead of just writing it, as a practical step. I regularly listen to Raidió na Gaeltachta as it helps to improve my

Irish. If we are serious about the language, we have to invest in it.

June 1992 saw the publication of the Green Paper which Séamus deliberately titled "Education for a Changing World". As with the pre-Easter document, he chose this time to release it as it was holiday time for teachers and would not impact on their classroom duties, and he asked for responses to come back in six months, which he felt was a very reasonable timeframe. But as usual, forces ranging from teachers to politicians complained bitterly that the six months timescale was "too restrictive". Fine Gael TD Jim Higgins appeared to echo the negativity which was beginning to creep in, and really got up Séamus's nose when he said "if the debate were to start in January and continue right through the school term until June, six months is extremely short in terms of providing adequate scope for a full debate". Séamus could not understand or accept this sort of procrastination. But when Jim Higgins went on to say that "it is certainly not adequate when one takes into consideration that the months of June, July and August have been lost", Séamus had the political equivalent of a seizure.

The Labour Party TD Brian O'Shea also made some comments, and initially appeared that he was not taking the same line as his Fine Gael colleague. He "complimented the minister on the way he introduced the debate" but went on to be equally critical of the document's June release saying that "in September, people are fresh in their minds after the summer break". Séamus felt this was the sort of talk that bedevilled progress, and only gave succour to those who wanted things to stay the same, regardless of the changing face of society. It was particularly galling for him to hear Opposition politicians effectively writing off the summer months at a time when their parties would attempt to portray the Dáil summer adjournment as a holiday. "It might be a holiday for them," he told me, "but ministers are usually at their desks for most of the summer, bar some time in August."

Introducing the 240 page Green Paper in Dáil Éireann on 16 October 1992, Séamus called the day long debate "historic" because of the scope and depth of the education issues involved and the national debate on whether education was a factor in restraining the Irish economy from the level of economic development and growth required. It was measure of his thoroughness that he arranged for a copy of the Green Paper to be sent to each Deputy and Senator in advance of the debate, and to each school in the State for the use of parents as well as teachers and management, as he truly wanted to get a consensus on the way forward for what was, and is still today, generally viewed as a world class education system.

In his introductory speech in Dáil Éireann, he honed in on the title of the Green Paper which was chosen to convey a fundamental reality that had to be confronted – that Ireland was undergoing some of the most rapid changes in its history, and was doing so in a world of ever accelerating change. The points made in that speech still have a resonance today:

> The speed of change is being caused largely by the creativity and enterprise of people in the developed countries. In the industrialised countries, wealth is now mostly created from invention, innovation, brain-power and knowledge. A nation's health is limited only by the imagination and enterprise of its people, and not by its natural resources. In this context, I make no apologies for wanting to provide balance and breath in education by emphasising science, technology, enterprise, and creative and critical thinking. I want the education system to play its full role in the development of the nation's people. I want the system to lead change into the next millennium, not simply to follow it. Education must continue to embrace the moral, spiritual, physical, aesthetic and intellectual development of students.

Going on to point out that the education system covered almost one million students, over 40,000 teachers and lecturers, and over 4,000 schools and colleges, he said that it "touched every home in the country", and that while Irish people value education, there would never be enough resources but "we will continue to invest in the education system, a system that receives 50 per cent of our total take from income tax". He made a critical point of acknowledging the investment "made by the parents of Ireland and by the Churches" and strongly believed that consensus on the way forward was the only pathway to "real and enduring change".

In a swipe at those in the political and educational world who would oppose for opposition sake, he said that:

> ... the achievement of consensus by definition requires a positive and dynamic contribution. It is not sufficient simply to knock proposals. I want to bring about real and tangible change where it matters. Unless what we do means improvement in quality and relevance of learning, it will be pointless. Since the publication of the Introduction to the Green Paper six months ago, I have sought to establish the widest possible consultation process. I want this process to be a model of openness in action, a headline of how a mature society debates an issue with fundamental and far-reaching implications for its future.

The Green Paper set out six key aims:

1. To establish greater equity in education

2. To broaden education so as to equip students more effectively for life, for work in an enterprise culture, and for citizenship of Europe

3. To make the best use of education resources by radically devolving administration, introducing the best management practice and strengthening policy-making

4. To train and develop teachers to equip them for a constantly changing environment

5. To create a system of effective quality assurance, and

6. To create openness and accountability throughout the system, and maximise parental involvement and choice.

It was intended as a serious document that effectively charted the process needed to bring education into the twenty-first century, following on from great advance made by previous Ministers for Education, such as Donagh O'Malley (uncle of former Fianna Fáil minister and Progressive Democrat founder, Des O'Malley) who introduced free secondary education in 1966; and before that Jack Lynch, who served just over two years from March 1957 to June 1959 and introduced education planning, rescinded the ban on married women teachers, amended the rules on corporal punishment and gave preferential funding for the growing technological area. The Lynch effect was crystallised in 1988 by Séamus O Buachalla who wrote in his document called *Education Policy in Twentieth Century Ireland* that "Mr Lynch was the first to link the functioning of the education system with the social reality of Irish society".

Also under discussion at that time, instigated by Séamus, was the proposition that university education should be free. This was not just an election gimmick. Knowing the value of third level education, Séamus wanted to ensure that those who now benefited from free primary and second level education would also have the chance to do more, regardless of their social background, which would in turn benefit Ireland and be a further significant social development in the Land of Saints and Scholars. In many ways, this thinking represented the new Ireland which had come from a predominantly insular agricultural base to an open, mixed economy in less than four decades.

Séamus always strived to get the broadest possible consensus and the possibility of free fees at third level was no different. One of his backroom associates, Eoin O'Brien, founder of the English Language Studies Institute, was "fundamentally opposed" to free fees across the board:

> Séamus was worried about the cost if it was to be introduced, and the negative vibes if it was not. What I recommended was to increase scholarships to cater for the best and the brightest from disadvantaged areas, along with helping their families who would otherwise expect their teenagers to go to work and contribute to the family budget.

However, once again political events dictated that Séamus would not be able to fully complete his ambitious programme and it was left to his successor, the Labour Party's Niamh Breathnach, to bring in a White Paper and to introduce free third level education. But Séamus was happy that he had "started the ball rolling" during just eleven months as Minister for Education and there would now be no turning back.

Chapter 5

A Step Back but Still a Minister

FORTUNATELY, OR UNFORTUNATELY (depending on your view), a general election to the twenty-seventh Dáil was held on 25 November 1992. With no party achieving an overall majority, the alternative for a Dáil unable to agree on a new Taoiseach and Government was very unpalatable and that thought tended to concentrate the collective minds of Fianna Fáil and Labour. No doubt, Fine Gael minds were of a similar view, but they needed Labour as well as others if they were going to have a realistic chance of getting into office. Séamus had fundamental misgivings about a coalition with Labour, believing that their ideology was not compatible with Fianna Fáil's, and as the National Director of Elections he had even gone so far as to publicly ridicule the idea before the election, along with other senior figures including Ray MacSharry, Padraig Flynn, Charlie McCreevy and David Andrews. But being the democratic pragmatist that he was, he was prepared to put those views aside in the interests of responding to the decision which the electorate had made. The outcome was the first ever coalition between Fianna Fáil and Labour with Albert Reynolds as Taoiseach and Dick Spring as Tanaiste.

That election saw two new faces joining Séamus Brennan in Dublin South's representation in the Dáil – Eithne Fitzgerald (Labour), who topped the poll with a remarkable 17,256 first preference votes, and Liz O'Donnell (Progressive Democrats), who took the fifth seat with 5,162 first preferences. Out was the Green Party's Roger Garland who secured less than half of his first preferences from two years previously, while Nuala Fennell (Fine Gael) had not contested the election.

On 12 January 1993, after just eleven months at the helm in Education, Taoiseach Albert Reynolds asked Séamus to become Minister for Commerce and Technology at the Department of Enterprise and Employment, where the senior minister was Labour's Ruairi Quinn from the neighbouring constituency of Dublin South-East.

This portfolio marked a return to the business and economic environment so beloved of Séamus. While he was disappointed not to have the senior ministry, Séamus was always a pragmatist and believed strongly that you move forward by taking the dice that are thrown to you, rather than by going off in a huff. While some of Séamus's local backroom supporters dithered about the post, some even suggesting he should refuse it, he went with the advice given by closer trusted allies and returned to the department where he began his ministerial career (albeit with an updated name – Industry and Commerce had become Enterprise and Employment.

Séamus immediately threw himself into his new responsibilities with his new Private Secretary, Kevin Doyle. Over the years, he had also got on well in a personal sense with Ruairi Quinn – perhaps Ruairi was not the usual Labour Party Minister with his Blackrock College Catholic upbringing and being a brother of the multi-millionaire businessman and former Chairman of AIB Bank, Lochlainn Quinn, as well as being a cousin of the Superquinn owner and Senator, Feargal Quinn.

Albert Reynolds was a man in a hurry, and in his capacity as President of Fianna Fáil he wanted to rejuvenate the party under his leadership and move away from the traumatic events surrounding his predecessor. He asked Séamus to take on the additional part-time role of Director of Organisation at Fianna Fáil headquarters, an unpaid post but designed to utilise the significant administrative and political skills which Séamus had demonstrated during his time as Fianna Fáil General Secretary under Jack Lynch (1973–1979) and briefly under Charlie Haughey

(1979). As usual, Séamus took on this task with great relish, working closely with the then General Secretary, Pat Farrell (who went on to become Chief Executive of the Irish Banking Federation) and served for two years until Albert Reynolds was succeeded as party President by Bertie Ahern, who promptly abolished the post of Director of Organisation as he felt it had run its course. To be fair, Séamus fully agreed with that analysis.

The Ministerial role of Commerce and Technology was characterised by the setting up of the Task Force on Small Business which marked the start of a new era when, for the first time, the central importance of small business as a creator of jobs got full recognition, along with the practical support and encouragement needed to play their full part in the nation's economy. In some ways, he saw this new role as a logical carry over from his time as Minister for Trade and Marketing (1987–1989) when the strategic role of marketing was first recognised.

With the full support of his senior minister, Ruairi Quinn, Séamus promptly assembled a group of small business practitioners who readily agreed to offer their services. He assigned around six months for the Task Force to come up with its recommendations – the "man of action" was in place again – as he did not believe in nor want a talking shop which sat for years and produced one or more reports which would end up gathering dust in a department storeroom. The importance of the Task Force was underlined when Séamus himself agreed to be the chairman at all meetings (see Appendix 2 for full list of membership).

The Task Force Report, containing 121 recommendations, was produced on time in March 1994. In his introduction to the report, Séamus said:

> Reports usually come first, followed (often too slowly) by action. This Task Force has broken that mould because already, important actions have flowed from its work. But the recommendations already accepted are only a small part of what is here, and what is here is in turn only a small part of what will eventually flow when new structures for small business are in place.

The Task Force had identified Ireland as a nation of small businesses, with some 98 per cent of non-farm businesses defined as small by virtue of having less than 50 employees and less than IR£3 million (€3.8 million) in turnover, accounting for around half of all employment in the private sector. It had further refined this figure to show that fewer than 10 people were employed in 90 per cent of enterprises. The recommendations were contained in what were described as five pillars:

- Raising money

- Rewarding risk

- Reducing burdens

- Providing help and

- A new deal for small business.

According to Task Force member Des Cummins, "the most significant of a range of significant measures was low interest fixed rate finance" for small business, which was seen as being more acceptable to business owners than outside equity and was more affordable than short-term debt. This plan was for £100 million (€127 million) to be available through the Small Business Expansion Loan Scheme operated by the State-owned bank, the Industrial Credit Corporation. The intention was for this fund to be supplemented by other banks, and within a short period AIB Bank and Bank of Ireland came in with matching amounts, joined later by Ulster Bank with a £50 million (€63.5 million) fund.

The Prompt Payments Act, by which all State bodies are required to pay their bills within a defined period, was also directly attributed to the work of the Task Force, and has been a major benefit to business. As Séamus said, "One of the lessons we learnt is that you can't make exactly the same rules for a company with 5,000 people as you can for a company with five people".

He had hoped to personally follow this landmark report with a variety of legislation where that was required, or a change in procedures where that would make a difference, but as so often happened in his political life, circumstances were to conspire which would deny Séamus the opportunity to complete his important work.

In November 1994, Tanaiste Dick Spring found a reason to invoke his idea of a rotating Taoiseach first suggested some years previously (the thinking in Fianna Fáil, which was rejected, was that he meant to rotate Fianna Fáil and Labour) when he led his Labour colleagues out of coalition with Fianna Fáil and into a Rainbow Coalition of Labour, Fine Gael and Democratic Left under John Bruton as Taoiseach. Spring's official reason for pulling out began over a lack of confidence in the Attorney-General, Harry Whelehan, which had been simmering for some time.

Seemingly the last straw for Spring was the failure of the Attorney-General to follow up an extradition warrant from May 1993 in regard to a former priest, Brendan Smyth, who was wanted in Northern Ireland on child sex abuse charges. Under Irish law, the Attorney-General is the person responsible for confirming extradition warrants. The matter came to public light after the Northern Ireland authorities sought an update on the extradition request, and this led to Opposition suggestions that the file had been lost or deliberately buried, an allegation which was strenuously denied. The charges went back almost 30 years and the view in the Attorney-General's office was that the details needed to be fully examined to ensure that a fair trial could take place in Northern Ireland if the warrant was endorsed.

On 25 October 1993, the Minister for Justice, Maire Geoghegan-Quinn, told the Dáil that the Attorney-General had not personally seen the file before the update request had come in. The following day, Chief Whip Noel Dempsey confirmed that a new protocol was now in place to ensure that all future extradition requests would be immediately notified directly to the Attorney-General himself.

On its own, this might have been enough for the Coalition partner. But the other element of this strange story is that Taoiseach Albert Reynolds insisted on appointing the Attorney-General to the newly vacant post of President of the High Court, despite the compelling objections of his Tanaiste, Dick Spring, over the extradition debacle. Reynolds felt obliged to make a statement in the Dáil to say that the appointment would not have been made "if I had known then what I know now", but he stopped short of suggesting that Whelehan might "step aside" (a phrase which had been used some years previously by Charlie Haughey in relation to controversy involving the then Chairman of An Post, Michael Smurfit; the then Chairman of the Custom House Docks Development Authority, Seamus Páircéir; and the then Chairman of Aer Rianta, Dermot Desmond).

But at this stage, the essential element of mutual trust between a Taoiseach and a coalition partner seemed to have irretrievably broken down. Stephen Collins, in *The Power Game*, recalled an emergency meeting of Fianna Fáil ministers on Monday, 14 November 1994, when Séamus informed his colleagues about contacts with Ruairi Quinn, Deputy Leader of the Labour Party and Séamus's then senior minister, with a possible solution for Reynolds:

> This involved the Taoiseach gorging himself on vast quantities of humble pie. He would have to come into the Dáil the following day and apologise to the Irish people for the handling of the Smyth case, promise a total reform of the Attorney General's office and under no circumstances defend the handling of the case by Whelehan. On top of that, he would have to pay tribute to the contribution of Dick Spring and Labour to the Government and express regret to Spring at the way he had broken trust.

Reynolds and some of his ministers felt that this demand was too much but still wanted to meet Labour half way. In their view, the word "apologise" was too strong, but the word "regret" was considered to be appropriate. All other elements were included in the script which Reynolds delivered.

But Labour saw it in a different light and walked out of Government with Fianna Fáil, and eventually into Government with Fine Gael and Democratic Left.

On losing the office of Taoiseach, Albert Reynolds resigned as leader of Fianna Fáil, and was succeeded by Bertie Ahern who had been nominated by Séamus at the Parliamentary Party meeting. The new leader was viewed as a person who would bring Fianna Fáil together again, although some still saw Bertie as a protégé of Charlie Haughey's. From Séamus's perspective, it was the first time in many years that "Fianna Fáil became a genuinely nice place with no dissent". Bertie had managed to reunite the various factions which had existed under Haughey and Reynolds so that there was now one party going forward. And this new era was copper fastened in subsequent elections when the figures showed that Fianna Fáil was getting more vote transfers because Bertie's uniting leadership style was more engaging for the electorate than that of his two predecessors.

While Bertie had been a staunch defender of Haughey, he had managed to simultaneously not fall foul of those who held a different view. It was clear that Bertie, as the new broom, would have to negotiate with Labour if there was to be any chance of the Government remaining in office with him as Taoiseach. And so he set up negotiating teams which included Séamus, Mary O'Rourke and Brian Cowen to discuss social welfare and tax issues with Ruairi Quinn, Brendan Howlin and Joan Burton.

At this stage, Fianna Fáil had become quite adept at negotiating for a coalition, with the experience of just 18 months previously still fresh in their minds. They knew the foibles of their erstwhile coalition bride and with the legendary skills of both Séamus and Bertie, they were going to go all out to resume political marital relations. But there was one occasion during the discussions, as there always is, when a particularly difficult issue was proving awkward for both negotiating teams. The Fianna Fáil team had to keep the line intact. There was no room for manoeuvre and, almost in exasperation, Séamus announced that he had his "riding instructions on this from Bertie".

Meanwhile, as the controversy over Harry Whelehan's appointment continued unabated, the newly appointed President of the High Court resigned six days later so as to keep direct politics out of the judiciary, but it was too late for Albert Reynolds, for Bertie Ahern, for Fianna Fáil, and for the Fianna Fáil/Labour Government. The negotiations broke down and Labour made their decision to go with Fine Gael and Democratic Left, a decision which would have a profound effect on the vote pattern for those parties for years afterwards.

To its credit, the succeeding Rainbow Government (1994–1997) continued to implement many of the recommendations from Séamus's Task Force on Small Business, and within two years well over half of the 121 recommendations were fully implemented and some of the remaining ones were partially implemented. Former Task Force member Des Cummins is adamant that "the proposals really worked because there was a defined list of things to do", rather than just a theoretical wish list. In his case, he was also able to "pursue the agenda through the Small Firms Association" of which he was a prominent member.

Chapter 6

In Opposition then Back to Cabinet

FOR THE FIRST TIME IN MANY YEARS, the Government of Ireland had changed without a general election taking place. Paraphrasing Albert Reynolds when he spoke about coalition with the Progressive Democrats some years before, Séamus Brennan was confident that the Rainbow would be only "a temporary little arrangement". Fianna Fáil went onto the Opposition benches and Séamus Brennan was appointed to the senior post of Front Bench Spokesman for Tourism, Transport and Communications, shadowing the new Fine Gael Minister, Michael Lowry, and marking a return to the area of responsibility he had as Minister for Tourism, Transport and Communications just a couple of years earlier.

But the sudden nature of the change of Government had more immediate effects on the personal staff of Séamus Brennan.

As an Opposition TD, he could only keep his Personal Secretary, Mary Browne, as she was part of his Oireachtas allowance. The Economic Adviser, Dick Doyle, went on to become the vibrant Chief Executive of Phonographic Performance Ireland (PPI), which is responsible for collecting and paying royalties to music artists. This author, a long-time Political Adviser, became a freelance journalist working with the *Evening Press*, *The Irish Press*, *Sunday World*, *The Irish Times*, RTÉ Radio, *Woman's Way*, and a number of smaller special interest magazines, while also continuing to help Séamus with constituency work. Séamus wanted to keep his personal team together as much as possible because of his strong intuition that there would be a general election within a couple of years and every effort would then be made to return to

Government at the earliest opportunity. He was to be proven right.

The choice of Séamus as Opposition Spokesman, shadowing the department where he had previously served as minister from 1989 to 1992, kept him at the forefront of public life and his frequent media appearances belied the fact that he was temporarily out of Government.

In the summer of 1996, Séamus received a copy of a frightening and unsolicited nine page letter from a senior Garda officer which starkly identified what was called an "alarming increase in the use of syringes in the commission of robberies, etc,". The letter went on to say that a syringe "has become the favourite weapon used by criminals in the course of aggravated crimes" and "could be regarded as having a greater long-term traumatic effect on victims than a gun or knife". Elsewhere in that letter was a breakdown of recorded statistics throughout the country showing that the use of syringes in crime over a period of three-and-a-half years from 1993 to the middle of 1996 had doubled. Half of the detailed letter suggested wording for new legislation to deal with the problem.

Given the source of the letter, Séamus could not ignore it and brought it to the attention of the Fianna Fáil Spokesman on Justice, John O'Donoghue, who was equally shocked. The result was a Fianna Fáil bill called the Punishment of Aggravated Robbery Bill, 1997, which was published on 25 February 1997. This was followed the next day by either a coincidence or the political equivalent of industrial espionage as the Minister for Justice, Nora Owen, published what John O'Donoghue described as the "miraculously produced Non-Fatal Offences against the Person Bill, 1997". Whatever the origin of the bill, it did result in legislation being enacted in May 1997, just before the Fine Gael/Labour/Democratic Left Government went out of office, which responded well to the letter that was originally sent to Séamus.

His forecast of the temporary nature of the Rainbow Government came to pass on 6 June 1997 with the general election to the twenty-eighth Dáil when the Rainbow was defeated and Fianna

Fáil went into Government with the Progressive Democrats and the support of four Independent Deputies: Jackie Healy-Rae, Harry Blaney, Tom Gildea, and Mildred Fox – who were to become known later as "Brennan's Babes" because of his crucial role in keeping them on the right side of the minority Government. The Taoiseach was Bertie Ahern and his Tanaiste was Mary Harney.

The Dublin South election saw the previous poll topper, Eithne Fitzgerald (Labour) lose her seat as her first preference vote tumbled from 17,256 to 6,147 – a remarkable downturn in just over four-and-a-half years. With Séamus, Tom Kitt, Alan Shatter (Fine Gael) and Liz O'Donnell (Progressive Democrats) all re-elected, the newcomer this time was Fine Gael's Olivia Mitchell, who increased her first preference vote by over 6,000 since the previous election.

Because Fianna Fáil was a minority Government, the new Taoiseach wanted the time to complete his programme and to ensure that he would confound the critics by serving the full five year term. On June 26, he asked Séamus Brennan to take on the critical task of Government Chief Whip, which although not a senior departmental post, gave him the all important seat at the cabinet table, day-to-day contact with the Parliamentary Party, opportunities to interact with the media, and the edge in the Dublin South constituency. His long official title was "Government Chief Whip, Minister of State at the Department of the Taoiseach and Minister of State at the Department of Defence with special responsibility for Civil Defence".

As previously, when he was appointed a junior minister after serving in a senior post, a couple of backroom supporters had urged Séamus to immediately reject any offer which was not a senior economic ministry. But he chose to ignore their advice. Having discussed the matter with more seasoned senior political associates, he accepted the Taoiseach's offer and moved into his new office on the ground floor of the Department of the Taoiseach. Once again, he had taken the pragmatic view that keeping a place at the cabinet table represented the best opportunity for future advancement in his ministerial career.

On the wall of his constituency office in Churchtown for many years was a cutting from an article by Martin McCormack in the *Evening Herald* from the early 1980s which carried the heading: "The Young Man Most Likely to be Taoiseach". While Séamus had harboured serious ambitions to be Taoiseach in his early political life, he had effectively gone off the concept by the mid-1990s because of the serious intrusion into the private life of anyone holding that office. He often commented to people privately that "it was intrusive enough being a minister without the all-embracing goldfish bowl of being the most senior person in the Government".

Harry McGee in *The Irish Times* recalled a time when he did a *Connacht Tribune* interview with Séamus:

> ... where he said his political dream was to arrive back in Galway in an open-topped car, like John F. Kennedy did, as Taoiseach. He never achieved that ambition and knew from mid-career that it would not be.

He now reconciled himself to the idea that the closest he would get to the Taoiseach's Department would be this post.

Within 24 hours of his appointment, he found himself travelling to Hong Kong to represent the Government at the official ceremony which returned Hong Kong to China. Having carried out that duty on behalf of the Government, he was back at his desk in Government Buildings a few days later to meet his new Private Secretary, Jennifer Masterson, who was later succeeded by Alice Kearney. The team of Mary Browne and this author moved seamlessly with Séamus to the Department of the Taoiseach, and very soon it seemed as if he had not been away from Government at all.

Once again, he threw himself into the new task of skilfully keeping the different strands of Government support in tune, carefully resolving minor hiccups before they had a chance to become major convulsions. Taoiseach Bertie Ahern had also previously served as Chief Whip so he knew the task from an insider's view, although he never had to contend with a minority Government. Séamus once described Bertie's period as Chief Whip in the following terms: "As Chief Whip, he learned to come down the white line and take both sides of the street with him – I don't know how he got away with it."

That was the scale of the task now facing Séamus, although it was a far more volatile situation than any previous Chief Whip ever had to face. But it was his universal popularity with political friend and foe alike that allowed him to enhance his long standing reputation as a calm, measured politician who could be relied upon in any crisis, to fix any problem and to bat for the Government in a coherent way no matter what the issue – "a safe pair of hands" as he was so often described.

But that image only partly portrays the real Séamus Brennan who always carried a range of economic statistics in his head, plans for improving legislation and infrastructure, and political facts about a myriad of constituencies and personalities. Journalists knew that he was never short of a reasoned opinion on the pressing issues of the day, which is what you expect from a serious senior politician, and as Chief Whip it was one of his responsibilities to brief the Pol Corrs (Political Correspondents) once a week, or more often if that was required. He was effectively the political equivalent of a Government Press Relations Officer, although the then Government Press Secretary, Joe Lennon, might look at it a bit differently. But Joe Lennon, as with all Government Press Secretaries, was seen as being effectively the Press Relations Officer for the Taoiseach of the day rather than for the Government as a whole. However it is viewed, journalists knew they could always rely on Séamus to give them their story of the day – very often after he had thought out several angles of the same story so that they could claim an "exclusive". Giving a journalist an "exclusive" was seen as the political counterpart of that journalist having a win on the Lotto.

While he had always been media-friendly, this weekly interaction with the Leinster House journalists gave him the unique opportunity to greatly enhance his reputation in that regard. He believed that by being open and approachable to the media, they would be open and fair in their reporting of the Government's activities and, by extension, the reporting of his own national and local political work. He subscribed to the quotation attributed to Irish author and dramatist, Brendan Behan (1923–1964), that "there is no such thing as bad publicity, except your own obituary". He also endorsed the saying, "a picture is worth a thousand words" – the origin of this saying is unknown, except that it appears to be American, first used in 1911 by a newspaper editor in an address to a Men's Club and taken up subsequently by various newspapers.

It was this openness to the media that allowed Séamus to achieve an enormous amount of coverage in both words and pictures in whatever capacity he served – coverage that was regularly the envy of his Government and Opposition colleagues who would often scratch their heads in amazement at why their own activities would often not get the same level of media interest. But the truth is that journalists liked Séamus because he rarely tried to pretend things were better than they were. He acknowledged when problems existed, instead of denying them, and his attitude was usually on the lines of "Yes, there is a problem, and here is what we are going to do about it". As Andrew Lynch noted in the *Evening Herald*, "This refreshing honesty meant that he was widely regarded as one of the good guys in Leinster House".

The downside, if there was one, of being so intimately familiar with the media was that in times of difficulty and controversy, Séamus was the senior person who was regularly asked to put his head above the parapet to provide a calming influence for the nation on whatever the pressing issue was. The view in Fianna Fáil and in Government appeared to be that "whenever there is trouble, send for Brennan".

Aside from all the serious stuff, Séamus also had a most wonderful sense of humour and could make a joke out of any simple statement which often served to ease the tension of a critical issue, whether that was with political opponents, the media, or irate constituents at a public meeting. He never personalised political opposition, preferring instead to concentrate on policy differences. That talent served him well as Government Chief Whip and effectively complemented the legendary negotiation skills of his boss,

Taoiseach Bertie Ahern. This trait also continued to serve him extremely well in the political and other roles he played over his Government lifetime.

On one particular occasion, a senior Minister was about to be engulfed in a major controversy. Séamus, the senior Minister, and Gerry Howlin (Special Adviser to the Taoiseach) met in the Chief Whip's office in Leinster House to go over what was expected to be a page or two of an official script which would be read into the Dáil record that day. But the minister in question arrived with a huge file and it was clear that he had not prepared the required and requested official script. This was a cause of some consternation in the room and Séamus said to the minister in his usual calm way: "There is a takeoff and a landing. The takeoff has gone smoothly – now don't f__ up the landing." Unfortunately, the record shows that the minister in question did "f__ up the landing" on that occasion but lived to fight another day.

The five years spent as Government Chief Whip are credited by commentators and historians alike as being singularly crucial to that Government serving its full term, a feat not achieved by many previous Governments. It was even more remarkable due to the minority status of that particular Government, and the vagaries of the four sensitive Independent Deputies who signed up with their support.

But in April 1999, for the second time in his ministerial career, Séamus narrowly missed becoming a casualty of the roads.

He was on his way to a function in Co. Kildare when a trainee Garda motorcyclist crashed into his official car being driven by Liam Farrell. Luckily, the motorcyclist had the good sense not to be on his bike at the time of impact and there was no injury to anyone, as the bike ended up beneath the car. This was a narrow escape for a man who was to go on to become the saviour of the roads as Minister for Transport in the new millennium.

Locally in Dublin South (which Séamus always called "the Premier Constituency"), four stalwarts of his former long-time constituency colleague Niall Andrews (who had retired from Dáil Éireann at the 1987 general election having been elected to the

European Parliament in 1984) were left without a local political home as Niall had decided to make his life as an MEP for Dublin. Paul McCormack, Tony Kelly, John Pollock and Des Brennan (collectively and very irreverently known locally as "the Bowery Boys") were invited by close associate Alan Elliott to join the Brennan team, a move which Séamus endorsed and warmly welcomed when they subsequently came on board. The Bowery Boys were called after a New York gang who often fought Irish gangs and were affiliated with a group called the "Know Nothing" political party which lasted from 1849 to 1856. But that irreverent title for fellow Fianna Fáil members was all in good fun.

With his work as Chief Whip in a minority Government, he did not have as much time as he wished to concentrate on the 1999 local elections. Nevertheless, he put special teams with his favoured candidates in the four electoral areas covering the Dublin South Dáil constituency. In the three-seat Stillorgan electoral area of Dun Laoghaire Rathdown County Council, he equally supported Senator Don Lydon and Gerry Horkan who both polled well, receiving in total between them almost 21 per cent of the valid poll. However, Lydon was the victor but would give up his seat to Horkan when the dual mandate was abolished four years later.

In Glencullen, Séamus supported former Councillor Jimmy Murphy, who was easily elected along with newcomer Maria Corrigan – a result which gave Fianna Fáil two out of three seats. Tragically, Murphy died three years later and was succeeded by his son, Tommy.

In the huge six-seat Dundrum electoral area, which included Séamus's Churchtown home and his constituency office, he saw two of his supporters being elected – outgoing Councillor Trevor Matthews and local activist Tony Kelly. The Kitt-supported candidate, outgoing Councillor Tony Fox, topped the poll with a whopping 21.67 per cent while his fellow outgoing Councillor, David Boylan (who was associated with former TD, Niall Andrews MEP), saw his support plummet and he lost out. Strangely enough, the new Fianna Fáil Councillor, Tony Kelly, had also been a close associate of Niall Andrews when Andrews was a local TD, but had been one of the Bowery Boys who came over to join Séamus's team.

Meanwhile, events were unfolding over in the seven-seat Terenure Rathfarnham electoral area of South Dublin County Council which would see Séamus's supported candidate Senator Ann Ormonde topping the poll and being joined on the Council by Tom Kitt's favourite, John Lahart, on his first outing.

On 20 October 1999, the death occurred of Séamus's mentor, Jack Lynch. Jack was the Fianna Fáil leader and Taoiseach who had given Séamus his first break in political life when he appointed him to be Fianna Fáil General Secretary at the age of 25. He subsequently appointed him to the Seanad after the spectacularly successful 1977 general election which saw Fianna Fáil return to power with a 20-seat majority – although in hindsight, a majority of that nature can be more problematic than a slim majority as Government Deputies can be less disciplined and more ready to take stands on issues that won't cause the Government to lose votes but which go down well in their constituencies. As Chief Whip, Séamus was glad that he did not have that "problem" this time.

Two of the significant high points of the five years in the Taoiseach's Department were the huge success of the National Millennium Committee (as Minister of State at the Department of the Taoiseach) and the transition of the Civil Defence organisation into a statutory body (as Minister of State at the Department of Defence).

With the increased workload needed for the National Millennium, Séamus secured Government approval to recruit the Deputy News Editor of the *Irish Independent*, Tom Rowley, as Press Officer to the soon to be constituted National Millennium Committee, and Laurie Cearr from RTÉ as the Committee's Marketing and Projects Manager. He was also given cabinet approval for this author to be promoted to Special Adviser, the first time a Government Chief Whip was given such assistance. The post of Personal Assistant was filled by the secondment of Bobby Holland from his position as a national teacher at Drimnagh Castle School in Dublin.

In the knowledge that the National Millennium would not come this way again for some 40 generations, Séamus was determined to reach out and involve everybody in the growing excitement and anticipation that this great benchmark in history was making – the transition from the twentieth century to the twenty-first.

Séamus wanted to select a committee which would be representative of business, the community and different political views – he also wanted to make it a committee with a strong hint of razzmatazz by including people involved in show business. With that brief in his head, he went about selecting and contacting the people who would collectively be known as the National Millennium Committee.

Deciding to chair the committee himself, he used the template of the proven structures for the Task Force on Small Business, which he had set up during his period as Minister for Commerce and Technology (1993–1994), and the National Marketing Group, which he had as Minister for Trade and Marketing (1987–1989). (See Appendix 2 for the full list of membership.)

This committee had responsibility for approving applications for Millennium funding from a budget of €33 million. Apart from the thousands of small allocations to projects and events the length and breadth of the country, its work will be most remembered for the Millennium Candle delivered to every home in the country (1.28 million homes), together with a scroll for an individual native Irish tree planted in State forests for each family – the People's Millennium Forests project. In Dublin, the Liffey Boardwalk began life as a Millennium-sponsored project costing IR£1.5 million (€1.9 million), and it has since been extended by Dublin City Council.

Other landmark projects were permanently illuminating prominent bridges in Dublin, Cork and Limerick; reintroducing Golden Eagles to Ireland; floodlighting churches; the Millennium Bridge in Galway City; Clyde Wharf Plaza in Waterford; refurbishment of the Gaiety Theatre; and many other projects which helped to bring the message to practically every town in Ireland,

and to Irish people abroad. In broad terms, the available funding was allocated to projects nationwide under the headings of Environment Projects; Arts, Education and Cultural Projects; Social Projects; Community Support Projects; Church/Christian Projects; Diaspora Projects; and Celebrating the Millennium.

The delivery of the candle was a monumental task in itself and could not have been achieved without the full and enthusiastic support of the workers in An Post. When a member of the public queried how the candle would fit into letterboxes, it was quickly demonstrated that the intention was to deliver it by hand with the postal worker knocking on the door. This was to make direct contact with individual households and to also avoid the potential for a domestic fire due to mishandling of the candle by it falling into a child's hands.

But even before the candle got into production, there were decisions to be made: the size of the candle, the type of wick to be used, the consistency of the wax – all of these led to a final interesting discussion among those in the Millennium Office. At a meeting the day before a scheduled formal meeting of the National Millennium Committee, it was necessary to have a recommendation on the candle. Various types and sizes of candle were laid out as the merits of each were discussed, and even Séamus's renowned patience was wearing thin: "I'm supposed to be in the middle of keeping the Government of the country going. I'm not supposed to be sitting here for hours talking about wax and wicks and the size of bloody candles". A recommendation was agreed five minutes later.

It was hoped that households throughout Ireland would light the candle at sunset on New Year's Eve in a huge act of joint celebration. Broadcaster Joe Duffy wrote in the official record of the Millennium, *The Millennium Legacy*:

> Like all great ideas, the Millennium Candle lit people's imagination. The small candle became a big idea. On New Year's Day, Liveline was the first live programme on RTE for the new millennium and what did our listeners

want to talk about? – The Millennium Candle. How it was such a brilliant idea. How it lit the spot. Simple ideas work with imagination. One match and the candle worked. One imagination and it lived, straddling two Millennia.

The ripples of the "small candle" were felt across the oceans and the continents. In a letter to *The Irish Times* on 14 January 2000, Mary Hatch of the Irish Women's Network of British Columbia in Vancouver wrote:

Asked to speak at the Nollaig na mBan dinner in a Vancouver hotel, I concluded my remarks by describing the candle ceremony at sunset on New Year's Eve in homes throughout Ireland. I then lit my candle, which I had brought back with me from Dublin, and was about to take it back to my table when it was taken from my hands. It was not returned to me until it had been held, with some emotion, by every one of the 120 women in the room.

The Liffey Boardwalk was in the sights of independent Senator David Norris who wrote in *The Millennium Legacy*:

I have strolled on the Boardwalk and I can testify that what looked initially a slightly daft idea is now a real success and well on the way to being adopted by Dubliners and tourists alike as one of the City's special treats.

But it was the project for planting trees that particularly captured the fertile imagination of actor Mick Lally:

All woods are romantic and Tourmakeady Wood is no different. It is commonly held that Éamonn de Valera and Sinead (Ni Fhlanagáin) would sojourn there when Sinead was teaching at the nearby Irish language Coláiste Chonnacht. Tourmakeady is now a People's

Millennium Wood – a far cry from its early days when, as
the private property of the local landlord, any incursion
by local peasantry was at best, discouraged, if not
actually forbidden.

The tree project also drew genuine praise from an unlikely
source – Patricia O'Donovan, former Deputy Secretary of the Irish
Congress of Trade Unions:

What made the project so wonderful was that it was all-
inclusive. Every household the length and breadth of the
country benefited from the event, including people who
did not fit the standard definition of a household.

This was one of the only times that Séamus would ever be
praised by a senior trade union official – if only he could have captured the spirit of that praise in the difficult times ahead.

But inevitably in any situation where thousands of projects and
events are being supported and funded, some will not fully step up
to the mark.

One idea which had to be ruled out was a fountain in Dublin
Bay – not just any old fountain mind you, but one which would
compare with the world's biggest and best like Geneva at 460 feet
and Jeddah at 753 feet. Alas, despite a substantial period of time
going on the research and consultations with the Port Authority, it
was not possible to proceed due to shipping lanes, tidal effects,
wind, etc.

Another slightly disappointing project was the production of
the Messiah XXI for the New Millennium. This was a modern arrangement of Handel's choral masterpiece by composer (and later
Progressive Democrat election candidate) Frank McNamara. The
Committee had felt that it was an appropriate modern day celebration of the two millennia anniversary of the birth of Christ and
was being recorded by RTÉ for broadcast at home and abroad.
There were also plans for the distribution of CDs and videos of the
event. A deal was done whereby IR£700,000 (€889,000) of the
estimated IR£2 million (€2.54 million) cost would be paid from

the Millennium fund and 10 per cent of all profits up to the State's contribution would be donated to charity. While the performance in Ireland received standing ovations, it never got to the stage of making the substantial profits which were expected – although it was seen on all continents bar Antarctica – but it was still a worthwhile project to have done.

On the music side, Séamus believed that he had a commitment from committee member and singer Ronan Keating to compose and release a special Millennium song, but as the Millennium date approached with no sign of the expected song, Séamus was forced to reluctantly give up on the idea, although he was bitterly disappointed by this and told me privately that he felt let down. It was suspected by those close to the Millennium that either Ronan or his management did not want to proceed with what they thought might conflict with his other musical commitments, but there was never any official explanation given to Séamus for the song's non-appearance – on the other hand, no funds were paid over either.

As always, there were some politicians who tried to capitalise in a negative way on the good work and good feeling which was in the country. An example of this was in July 2000 when one-term Fine Gael Councillor Eoin Costello felt that Dun Laoghaire Rathdown was "comprehensively ignored" and that he was "incensed", despite his own figures showing that the area had received support for 79 local projects apart from sharing in national projects. The Councillor even referred to Séamus as being a representative of Dublin South, which is correct in one sense, but not in the way suggested by the former Councillor. It appeared that he chose to ignore the fact that the Dun Laoghaire Rathdown County Council area incorporates most of the Dublin South Dáil constituency (the Rathdown portion) – or perhaps he was just reflecting the old mentality that thought Dun Laoghaire was still an independent Borough Council. In any event, the National Millennium Committee were not concerned about constituency boundaries – their job was to support appropriate projects which would not otherwise be done and which would be seen in the future as significant legacies of the whole Millennium celebration.

All over Ireland, there is continued evidence of projects which were supported by Millennium funding and are an enduring legacy into the twenty-first century. When it was all over, Séamus jokingly said: "That was most enjoyable, but I'm not doing the next one!"

All Chief Whips also have the title of Minister of State for Defence. In that role, Séamus had a second Private Secretary from that department, Gabriel Bradley, who was succeeded later by Bernie Maguire. At this particular time, the Minister for Defence, Michael Smith, officially delegated responsibility for the Civil Defence organisation to his Minister of State. Civil Defence was originally set up in 1950 during the time of the Cold War as part of a civil response to potential hazards which might arise in a nuclear situation. Its role was designed to be non-combatant and to undertake activities and measures which would help persons and property at a time of emergency. With some 6,000 members voluntarily making themselves available, Séamus had the goal of developing Civil Defence as a top class, second line emergency service. He felt it was time to bring the organisation into a full State authority with its own board, although not all in the top echelons of the Department of Defence agreed with this approach.

However, with the active support of his senior minister, and the assistance of Private Secretary Gabriel Bradley, a Civil Defence Bill was prepared and guided through the Oireachtas. It was described at the time as "the most important piece of Civil Defence legislation to be enacted in over 50 years". On 12 April 2002, it was signed into law by President Mary McAleese as the Civil Defence Act.

The new Civil Defence Board, under its first chairman, Dr. Michael Ryan from Limerick, took up office in June 2002 (see Appendix 2 for full list of membership). This marked the start of Civil Defence coming out of the shadows to take a full and more publicly recognised part of the uniformed branches of the State, fully equipped to take on its traditional role in twenty-first century Ireland.

There was an expected mid-term reshuffle of ministers in January 2000, with a lot of media speculation on Séamus being given a senior ministry in recognition of his work as Government Chief Whip. It was a fairly standard protocol that a serving Government Chief Whip had first call on any full cabinet vacancy arising during the term of office. However, it was not to be on this occasion, and although disappointed, Séamus was happy to bide his time while reflecting on the glow which had followed the successful National Millennium celebrations.

When Bertie Ahern rose in the Dáil to announce his revised line-up, he made what Senan Molony, Political Correspondent of the *Irish Independent*, described as "an unprecedented aside". The Taoiseach referred to Séamus's "strong claim to return to a departmental ministry", spoke of his "long political experience of great value to the cabinet", and uniquely described him as "indispensable" to the functioning of the whole Dáil. With that glowing tribute, Séamus could only bite his lip and continue working as Government Chief Whip – or as some called him, "Chief Shepherd of the Independents".

Meanwhile, local issues were demanding more and more of Séamus's attention. One such was the long-held plan for an 11 kilometre Eastern Motorway providing north/south road connection (other than the plans for a more westerly M50) which would complete the road infrastructure from Dublin Port to the M50. During his first period as Minister for Transport, road development had been the responsibility of the Minister for the Environment and Local Government, rather than the Minister for Transport – a situation which was rectified when Séamus became Minister for Transport for the second time in 2002. The plan for this road was initially conceived by Dublin Corporation in the 1970s, but in November 1992, the Environment Minister, Michael Smith, had announced that it would not proceed.

However, within eight years, it again figured in four plans drawn up for the Dublin City Development Plan, Strategic Planning Guidelines for Dublin, the Dublin Transportation Office's Platform for Change and a Report on National Development Priorities. It was against this backdrop that the Minister for the Environment in 2000, Noel Dempsey, conceded that it would be inappropriate to exclude the Eastern Motorway from development plans, a point which had been vigorously made to him by Séamus at an earlier special meeting. But today, the "plans" remain just that. While the reservation remains largely intact and sterilised, no firm decision has yet been taken as to when, or if, the work will proceed.

But this period also saw Séamus Brennan becoming the victim of the first of several attempts to smear him – an unfortunate and regrettable side effect of being a successful politician. Queries from *The Sunday Times* on 27 February 1999 (relating to a story reported in *The Sunday Tribune* in October 1993 which became the subject of legal proceedings) suggested that a financial contribution received during the 1987 election period was inappropriate, given that the contributor, Brendan Hynes, was Chief Executive of Tara Mines Ltd. at the time and was subsequently appointed for a short time as Chairman of Telecom Éireann (he later resigned over a dispute with the Government of which Séamus was a member).

However, the contribution, from a close friend of some 20 years standing, was shown to be fully in order as a personal, and not a company, contribution. A statement issued to the media by Séamus on 27 February 1999 said:

> I made it clear at the time that I had no connections with the company, nor had I received any donations from them to my knowledge. I am responding to the issue now because I believe it is politically important to do so and I have always felt strongly about protecting my personal integrity. There was nothing inappropriate in Brendan's personal support and it was treated as a normal election expenses contribution, used by my Election Committee specifically for such expenses as posters, leaflets, canvassers' meals, petrol, printing, local newspaper advertising, etc. There was no personal gain to me whatsoever.

While it was strange that a two-year-old story, subsequently shown to be false, had been carried in *The Sunday Tribune* in the first place (given that Brendan Hynes had for many years been a director of that paper, although he had significant differences over its editorial direction), it was extraordinary that it should resurface four years later for no apparent reason. Séamus had a personal view, which this author is aware of, on how it had come up again after four years, but libel laws prevent going into further detail as insufficient legal evidence currently exists as to its source. But it is clear that this was a deliberate attempt by a person or persons unknown to damage Séamus in his ministerial career.

Three months later, on 30 May 1999, a second smear attempt was made in a story reported in the *Sunday Business Post* that Séamus had received an interest-free loan from Bank of Ireland in 1986, and that an outstanding balance of IR£800 (€1,015) was written off in 1998. Séamus issued a strongly worded statement later that day:

> The story about me in today's *Sunday Business Post* is most unfair and deliberately seeks to create the wrong impression and undermine my good name.
>
> The bank account was an ordinary current account into which I would lodge my salary and from which I would pay my family expenses. I operated it for about fifteen years – and like many people, was in and out of overdraft. Full interest accrued on overdraft periods and from memory, in about 1985, I moved my account to Dublin, and at that time, the account had an overdraft of about IR£12,000 (€15,200)
>
> The Bank agreed to accept a repayment schedule on this of approximately IR£1,200 (€1,523) a year until the overdraft was cleared. The account is now cleared. Repayments were made for approximately 12 years and I did not concern myself as to the breakdown between interest and capital. Nor did I negotiate or become aware of any write off.

> There was no political aspect to this. I was a newly elected backbencher. As far as the bank was concerned, and as far as I was concerned, the scheduled repayments fully dealt with the matter.
>
> I am deeply offended at this invasion of my ordinary private domestic current account and somewhat disillusioned that such lengths are now being gone to, to undermine the good name of public representatives.

That statement should have been enough to deal with the issue, but Séamus was determined to get further backup for it as he was not prepared to have any suggestion of impropriety hanging over him. On 3 June 1999, Pat McDowell, Chief Executive, Retail Division, Bank of Ireland Group, wrote a letter which has never before been published but which was sent to the Public Offices Commission on 9 July 1999 as a matter of record. That letter said in its entirety:

> We were very disturbed indeed that details of your personal affairs with Bank of Ireland were placed in the public domain. We have not, so far, been able to determine how this occurred but I can assure you that the matter will be fully investigated.
>
> The inferences contained in the article in the *Sunday Business Post* regarding the Bank's handling of your account are entirely wrong and quite unjust to you. I am happy to confirm that there is no evidence whatsoever of any pressure ever being brought to bear on the Bank by you or on your behalf since your personal account was first opened in 1977. Your accounts were managed by the Bank fully in accordance with our normal practice. No special treatment was afforded to you and I have noted that you were, in fact, treated less leniently than other customers.

The balance (of £800) was not written off, as suggested by the *Sunday Business Post*.

We are happy to take any steps within our power to correct the misinformation that has been published.

With that irrefutable information, the story died as quickly as it had arisen. But whether it was one person or more responsible for the two smear attempts, there was going to be another attempt before too long.

Chapter 7

Roads and Trains and Planes

THE GENERAL ELECTION OF 17 MAY 2002 to the twenty-ninth Dáil marked the end of Bertie Ahern's first full five years as Taoiseach, the initial goal he had set for himself back in June 1997. The theme for Fianna Fáil at the election was "A lot done ... more to do" and the generation of this slogan has been credited to Séamus's friend, Bob Manson Sr., when it was being discussed with US political consultants at a Dublin hotel in the run-up to the election.

In Dublin South, Séamus topped the poll with 9,326 first preference votes and was joined by three of the other four outgoing TDs – Tom Kitt (7,744), Liz O'Donnell (8,288) and Olivia Mitchell (5,568) – but the well known volatility of the last seat resulted in the Green Party's Eamon Ryan (5,222) eclipsing Fine Gael's Alan Shatter (5,363) after transfers were taken into account. The effect of this remarkable result was that the first three seats were taken by outgoing Government TDs who were all ministers in the Government.

It was now clear that the huge success of Séamus's varied work at the Departments of the Taoiseach and Defence could not be ignored. His crucial role in keeping the minority Government in office for a full term had its reward when he was nominated on June 6 to serve as Minister for Transport in Bertie Ahern's second administration. His post as Government Chief Whip was taken over by Mary Hanafin from the neighbouring Dun Laoghaire constituency, who would hold the position until she was appointed Minister for Education in September 2004. Coincidentally, her successor was

Séamus's constituency colleague, Tom Kitt. It was rumoured at the time that the current Finance Minister, Brian Lenihan, was initially offered the job of Government Chief Whip but turned it down, preferring instead to become Minister for Children.

In Transport for the second time, Séamus felt as if all his dreams had come true yet again, giving him the opportunity to pick up his reforming plans where he had left off when he last held the Transport brief. His new Private Secretary was Roger Harrington who was succeeded by Dermot Murphy. This time around, it was a Department with a new name (having previously been the Department of Public Enterprise and the Marine under Mary O'Rourke). His personal staff of this author, Mary Browne, Tom Rowley and Bobby Holland had also packed up from their successful stint at Government Buildings and moved the short distance to Kildare Street at the corner of Setanta Place.

The Department of Transport also had a new Secretary-General in Julie O'Neill (the first woman to attain the rank of Secretary-General) and an expanded role. Under its previous incarnation, the department was responsible for aviation, road and rail transport, national roads and the Marine. The new department retained these functions with the exception of the Marine, but had additional responsibility for non-national roads and for taxis, both of which previously were in the Department of the Environment. Marine was inexplicably linked up to the Department of Communications and Natural Resources under Minister Dermot Ahern, which was indeed a bit of a puzzle. Séamus believed it would have fitted in better as part of Transport and would have led to a more holistic Department. As it happens, Marine did come back to Transport five years later when Noel Dempsey was in charge, but that was more to do with not giving it to the Green Party Minister, Eamon Ryan, who instead had Communications, Energy and Natural Resources.

It was probably a blessing that the two people at the helm of the new department were also new and came without any baggage from the outgoing administration. They were seen as a marvellous team and achieved extraordinary things during the short two-and-a half-years they served together. Séamus thoroughly relished having this portfolio for the second time and in Miriam Donohoe's *Irish Times* column headed "Brownie, not penalty points for Brennan", she wrote that "an enthusiastic Mr. Brennan nearly broke all the speed limits himself in his enthusiasm to get on with the job of being minister". In a similar vein, Niamh Connolly in *The Sunday Business Post* reminded the nation that Séamus was "referred to as the 'Duracell Bunny' – just wind him up and he sets to work".

His first official function was to welcome the inaugural flight of the new Air Canada scheduled service (Flight 894) between Toronto and Dublin/Shannon which began on 14 June 2002 after an absence of 23 years. At the ceremony in Dublin Airport, he gave an indication of his future thinking, returning to the aviation policy he pursued when he previously served as Transport Minister:

> The Government's aviation policy will focus on as wide a range as possible of reliable, regular and competitive air services to and from Ireland. I firmly believe that as an island nation, it is vital that we encourage a competitive and efficient network of air links to develop.

That line of thought could just as easily apply to his thoughts on land-based transport, which he outlined later that year when he cited plans to liberalise the public transport market in Ireland – plans which would ultimately fall foul of the trade unions and, more importantly, would lead to Taoiseach Bertie Ahern appearing to row back on assumed support for proposals which were deemed to be too revolutionary for his trade union friends.

Soon after, Séamus noticed that Dublin City Council had erected some new and strange road signage in the city centre and on learning that there had been no consultation with his department, he ordered the signs to be taken down and replaced with more readable versions. The signs had been described as "bewildering" and the instruction to the City Council gave a significant boost to his reputation as a doer, or as Niamh Connolly in The

Sunday Business Post Online (ThePost.ie) said, "his Action Man image".

This image was again portrayed in relation to a stretch of road in Co. Galway known today as the Loughrea By-pass. The land on which this road is built was privately owned and the local community had agitated for a by-pass for some years. The National Roads Authority had therefore negotiated for its purchase at agricultural land prices. But shortly before documentation was signed, Loughrea Town Council agreed to rezone the land as industrial on the basis that it was adjacent to an existing industrial zone. The effect of this would be to greatly enhance its value to the owner, and the National Roads Authority (also known as the taxpayer) would be forced to pay a much higher price to allow the planned by-pass to be built. Séamus was dismayed at this news and immediately instructed this author, his Special Adviser, to convey the word to the Council Chair that if the rezoning was not rescinded immediately, the plan for the by-pass would be scrapped.

This action had the desired effect, and shortly afterwards the Council agreed to rescind the earlier decision and restore the land to its previous zoning of agricultural. The National Roads Authority then moved quickly to acquire the land and put the project out to tender. When work was about to start, Séamus was on hand to officially turn the first sod but its official opening would be left to his successor, Noel Dempsey. Nevertheless, he was pleased that the desired outcome had been achieved and this small by-pass is a testament to his work in thwarting what was a rather strange move by Loughrea Town Council.

But within a couple of months of having settled back into reform mode in his beloved Transport, Séamus was about to be the target of unusual correspondence from a semi-state chief, Noel Hanlon, Chairman of Aer Rianta.

Having posed for photographs with Hanlon a short while before at the opening of the new €122 million terminal extension at Dublin Airport, Séamus was surprised to receive a typed letter accompanied by a cartoon, which *The Sunday Business Post* later exclusively revealed was of the former Canadian Prime Minister,

Brian Mulroney, welcoming passengers to "Friends of Mulroney Airport – dedicated to lining a few pockets – not the public purse – let us take you for a ride." Niamh Connolly, writing some months later in *The Sunday Business Post*, said that this was:

> ... a stark warning to the minister. Hanlon, not known for mincing his words, said that Toronto Airport was the only airport to embark on a policy of building an independent terminal, and it nearly brought down the Government.

Here was a semi-state chairman, appointed by the Government on several occasions to a variety of state boards, suggesting what could be interpreted as veiled threats to undermine a democratic Government's plans to provide a second terminal at Dublin Airport – could the relationship between chairman and minister ever be the same again?

In late October, *The Sunday Business Post* had a story about what their reporter, Niamh Connolly, called "a head-to-head clash at the Department of Transport" between Séamus and Noel Hanlon. Séamus made it very clear to the chairman that he expected Aer Rianta to stand up for itself and to protect the company:

> But if that turns into undermining Government policy, then I have a problem. If Ryanair, Aer Rianta or Aer Lingus have a problem, I expect them to make their views known, but none of them are entitled to undermine the Programme for Government.

Built into the Programme for Government were a number of items that Aer Rianta, or more specifically their chairman, had issues with:

1. The building of a low cost facility at Dublin Airport without delay

2. Examining proposals for a new independent terminal at Dublin Airport, and acting on them if the evidence suggests that such a terminal would deliver significant benefits

*Séamus with his mother,
Tess, 1949*

*Séamus and his sister Carmel at her
First Communion in 1953*

*Séamus's First Holy
Communion, 1955*

*Séamus (on right) with his Uncle
Pat Brennan and brother Joe in
Salthill, 1962*

Séamus (front left) with parents Jim and Tess Brennan and brother Joe in 1955

With mother Tess on a trip to Dublin in 1957

Séamus at school, 1958

The Brennan family in 1962 – Séamus is on the right

SLICK STUDENTS

*During soccer playing days as a student at UCG –
Séamus is third from the left in the front row, while Pat Rabbitte is
second from the right in the back row*

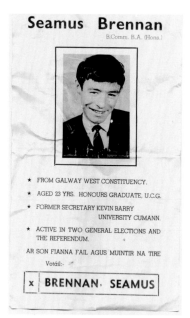

*First election poster (for
Fianna Fáil National
Executive, 1971)*

*First general election canvas
card (1981)*

Celebrating his successful election to the 22nd Dáil, June 1981

Receiving his first seal of office as a senior Minister (Tourism and Transport) in 1989 from President Paddy Hillery, with Taoiseach Charlie Haughey

Overseeing new radar installation at Dublin Airport as Minister for Tourism, Transport and Communications, 1991

Election poster, 1993

The golfer, after a bad putt

Surveying the "Premier Constituency", June 1990

"Confession" with Cardinal Desmond Connell, 2001

Stone plaque commemorating one of the National Millennium Projects, June 2001

The first Luas, 2004 – driver Eddie Byrne is a grandson of one of the last drivers on the old Harcourt Street Railway

Addressing the United Nations General Assembly in New York, 2004

3. Reorganising Aer Rianta and, as part of this process, ensuring that Shannon and Cork Airports have greater autonomy and independence.

Clearly, Séamus would have to get his "ducks in a row", as he often said. It was not going to be possible to do everything together and a political decision had to be made – go with an independent terminal or reorganise Aer Rianta.

The terminal issue boiled down to whether it would be built by the private sector, at no cost to the taxpayer, or whether it would be built at the State's expense. The Aer Rianta issue could be resolved by legislation and it made sense to get that out of the way before deciding on the ownership of any terminal. Once he made the decision to pursue the Aer Rianta reorganisation first, he threw himself into it wholeheartedly, while putting the terminal issue on the back burner, though still simmering.

The previous Minister, Mary O'Rourke, had strongly supported plans to float Aer Rianta on the Stock Exchange, as she had done with Telecom Éireann, which would have seen the publicly owned airports taken into private hands. But despite his capitalist profile and his reputation for generally being in favour of selling State companies, Séamus was totally opposed to any float of Aer Rianta and formally abandoned the O'Rourke plan saying that "vital public infrastructure should remain in State hands". He was also acutely conscious that Mary O'Rourke's previous floating of Telecom Éireann had been a major disaster for the mostly small shareholders who had been promised great things and who had been left nursing what were, for the bulk of shareholders, significant losses. Séamus equated selling Aer Rianta with selling public roads and public footpaths.

It was against this reforming backdrop that there was another shadow about to come on the horizon which some people clearly thought would dampen the highly regarded reputation of "Action Man". The dark underbelly of shadowy people who would stop at nothing to throw dirt around, on the basis that some of it might stick whether it was true or not, came into view again less than six months into this new Ministry. On 24 November 2002, the third attempt was made to smear Séamus.

An allegation, reported by Jody Corcoran in the *Sunday Independent* and repeated in the same paper on 1 December 2002, was made that €5,000 worth of brandy and cigars was procured from Aer Rianta (which had responsibility for the duty free shops at Dublin Airport) in the late 1990s when Séamus was previously Minister for Transport and that the bill was never paid. The article gave several conflicting stories that two senior executives in Aer Rianta had allegedly been aware of information, Chief Executive John Burke and former Chief Executive Derek Keogh; that the Aer Rianta Chairman, Noel Hanlon, had "provided most of the details"; and that board member Dermot O'Leary was also in the mix. This *Sunday Independent* "exclusive" was also picked up by RTÉ on 25 November 2002 when Charlie Bird interviewed Derek Keogh.

This was by far the most serious attempt to put a slur on Séamus's reputation, and on the day of publication he did two things. He immediately instructed his Secretary-General, Julie O'Neill, to carry out a full investigation, also giving a public assurance that once the report was completed, it would immediately be made public; and he issued a strong, clear and credible denial of the allegation. Aer Rianta also began its own investigation of the allegation to be carried out by their Chairman of Internal Audit, Tony Sweeney, and their Company Secretary, Brian Hampson.

This was not what Séamus had come into public life to do and he deeply resented the antics of those who adopted smear tactics in pursuit of their own anti-democratic ideology. "Let them come into the open, take off their Ku Klux Klan masks and put themselves before the public as I and my colleagues did," was his private response to me.

A lengthy editorial in the *Irish Independent* on 27 November 2002 concentrated on the origin of the allegation:

> The evidence available last night suggested a story deliberately 'planted' with the intention of smearing the minister. If that assumption is correct, it was a strange

tactic to base it on events that allegedly occurred many years ago and its purpose remains unclear.

The editorial went on to identify speculation about the proposals for the future of Aer Rianta as having a connection saying that these issues were "a matter of great commercial – and national – importance. It should be seriously and carefully argued, not made the subject of smears."

Drawing on another angle, the *Irish Independent* editorial said:

> Another aspect of the affair provides food for thought, and anxiety. Such is the current mood that many people, perhaps most people, are willing to believe charges resting on no better ground than that 'somebody thought he remembered something about something'. Once we lived in a culture of concealment. Now we live in a tribunal culture. The way for those in public life to combat it is to keep their reputations so bright that if they are forced to deny a rumour, the denial will be as firm and credible as that of yesterday.

Within five days, both investigations were completed, including a review by the Aer Rianta auditors KPMG, and not one single shred of evidence to support the allegation was found. According to Aer Rianta Chairman Noel Hanlon, the inquiry had "not seen any evidence which would substantiate the allegations contained in the *Sunday Independent*".

Whoever was responsible, the public release of the Inquiry Report put paid to their dirty tactics. The full text of the report is reproduced here as a matter of public record:

Inquiry into Allegations Published in the Sunday Independent on 24 November 2002

1. Background

On 24 November 2002, the Minister for Transport, Mr Séamus Brennan TD, instructed me to carry out a full investigation to establish the facts pertaining to allegations contained in an article published in the *Sunday Independent* that day headed 'Politician in Christmas Gifts Scandal'. The article claimed that a senior government politician left unpaid a €5,000 bill for whisky, brandy and cigars, allegedly delivered to his office in a van by Aer Rianta in the 1990s. It was claimed that the bill remains unpaid even though at least three invoices were sent. A copy of the article is attached at Appendix A.

Minister Brennan confirmed to me that he was the politician at the centre of the allegations. Minister Brennan last discharged the functions of Minister for Transport between July 1989 and February 1992.

2. Internal Investigation in Department of Transport

On Monday, 25 November, I initiated an investigation within the Department of Transport, to establish the facts, as they pertained to the Department, in respect of the allegations contained in the *Sunday Independent* article and any records held in the Department relating to these matters.

The internal investigation focussed on identifying any documentary evidence or other knowledge of:

Goods ordered from Aer Rianta, by or purportedly on behalf of the Minister or the Department, for which payment was not received by Aer Rianta, indicating the dates, items and costs involved and whether the goods were duty free or duty paid;

Any such goods delivered to the Department, the Minister, or any other person on his behalf, indicating the dates, locations and items involved and any receipts acknowledging delivery;

Invoices sent in respect of such goods indicating to whom and where they were addressed and the dates involved;

Correspondence with the Department, the Minister or any person purporting to act on his behalf in respect of such invoices and any debt arising in this context.

3. Trawl of Department of Transport Records

A comprehensive trawl of Department of Transport records since July 1989 was undertaken by staff of the Finance Unit of the Department. This included paper records up to 1992 and electronic records from October 1991. This trawl has shown no record of any outstanding invoice from Aer Rianta.

Outstanding invoices from any company in the range €4,000 to €5,500 were also checked but do not relate to whiskey, brandy, cigars or similar goods.

Payments to Aer Rianta in the range €4,000 to €5,500 were also checked and do not relate to whiskey, brandy cigars or similar goods.

Any invoices and payments in relation to whiskey, brandy, cigars or similar were also checked and were in order. These relate to relatively small purchases of up to about €300 in respect of official entertainment.

4. Interviews with officials of the then Department of Transport and the Minister's Personal Staff

The Assistant Secretary responsible for Corporate Services in the Department of Transport interviewed the following persons:

Officials who acted as Private Secretary to the Minister during the period 1989 to 1992 and for his immediate successor as Minister;

The Principal Officer in charge of the Finance Unit over the period from 1989 to 1992;

The Advisor, Personal Secretary and Personal Assistant to Minister Brennan during his term of office from 1989 to 1992.

None of the persons interviewed had any awareness or recollection of documents or incidents of the nature referred to in the *Sunday Independent* article.

I contacted all former Secretaries General for the Department of Transport for the period from 1989 to 2000. All were certain that they were not aware of any of the matters alleged in the article or of any issue involving the ordering, delivery or invoicing of goods to the Minister or the Department by Aer Rianta or of any outstanding debt to Aer Rianta.

All other current staff of the Department of Transport were contacted by email to ask if they had any information in relation to the delivery of such goods or are aware of any document – e.g. delivery dockets, invoices or receipts which might be relevant. No additional information was received on foot of this email.

5. Summary of Departmental Investigation

Following extensive enquiries by Finance Division staff, the Assistant Secretary responsible for Corporate Services and myself over the past five days, I have found no documentary or other evidence that might relate to an incident of the nature referred to in the *Sunday Independent* article.

6. Separate Investigation by Aer Rianta

On Monday 25 November I wrote to Mr John Burke, Chief Executive of Aer Rianta, asking him to provide a report dealing with the allegations which were the subject of the *Sunday Independent* article.

In a letter to me today (29 November), Mr Burke has stated that the Aer Rianta inquiry is almost completed and that they have seen no evidence or documentation supporting these allegations.

The Aer Rianta inquiry is expected to be completed early next week when a report from the Auditors to Aer Rianta will be provided to the Chairman. Aer Rianta have indicated that they do not expect that there will be any change in this position.

Julie O'Neill
Secretary General
29 November 2002

As far as Séamus was concerned, this was now a "clear and decisive result". He had spent a very trying week knowing that he was not guilty of any wrongdoing, but unable to clear himself before the reports came back. "Public life is difficult, whichever side you are on," he said, "and to have your integrity questioned is deeply upsetting and hurtful."

On 30 November 2002, Derek Keogh issued a statement which read:

Firstly, I want to welcome the fact that the two investigations have exonerated Minister Brennan. I also want to state that I have never had knowledge of a significant unpaid debt involving Minister Brennan and Aer Rianta, nor did I ever suggest to anyone that such a debt existed.

John Burke also denied having any knowledge or information, as did Dermot O'Leary, who insisted that he never made any allegations but only repeated what he had heard.

This led to three questions that were posed by Niamh Connolly in The Sunday Business Post Online (ThePost.ie):

Why the claims should take 12 years to enter the public domain? Why should the issue surface now? Whose interests were served by leaking such damaging claims that, if true, could only mean resignation for the minister?

As this had happened at a time when Séamus Brennan was beginning to re-initiate his consideration of major reform proposals for the semi-state bodies under his control, many believed (and

still do to this day) that a very deliberate campaign had been un-
derway to damage the minister in his political career and thereby
scupper reform plans. But the perpetrator or perpetrators appeared to fade away as the third defeat of dirty tactics gave them
no credibility. Shane Ross, writing in his column in the *Sunday
Independent* on 1 December 2002 under the caption "Brennan set
to slay dinosaurs", said:

> Aer Rianta is a Fianna Fáil fiefdom. Séamus Brennan is a
> loyal member of Fianna Fáil. When a loyal member of
> the tribe begins to trick around with one of his Party's
> sinecures, resistance can be fierce. Séamus, the
> politician, was naively trying to make Aer Rianta behave
> like a business. Aer Rianta has always been riddled with
> political animals. And they expect their ministers to
> understand the rules. Séamus didn't play and introduced
> his own. He has hopefully stared down the faceless
> cowards who tried to preserve their empire by toppling a
> minister.

In the same paper that day, John Drennan wrote that "the
smart money is on Séamus being the innocent victim of a drive-by
shooting in a semi-state power struggle".

Meanwhile, Jody Corcoran had indicated in his second article
that the source was what he called "a senior Fianna Fáil politician". But an editorial in the *Irish Independent* on 3 December
2002 noted that "the suspicion remains, especially in Government
circles that it (the smear) came from someone with Aer Rianta
connections", a suggestion that was consistently rejected by Aer
Rianta and its chairman.

Attempt three at smearing Séamus was shown to be dead in
the water and the important work which he had to do could now
resume in full flight. While he would have relished being able to
discover concrete proof of who was behind the smear, he knew
that such things happen with the territory. As Justine McCarthy
had written in the *Irish Independent* on 30 November 2002, "Like
any seasoned politician, he has his shoal of enemies, compounded

by the trail of bruised vanities he left behind the last time he held the Transport portfolio".

But Nick Webb in the *Sunday Independent* on 1 December 2002 went further. He said that:

> ... embattled Transport Minister Séamus Brennan has rattled a few cages since taking up office four months ago. He's taken on some of the inefficient semi-state bodies and he's also shoved the unions around. There is no doubt that Brennan has made enemies, some very serial whingers, but others very powerful and very dangerous.

On 8 December 2002, the original reporter of the story, Jody Corcoran, wrote for the third consecutive week in the *Sunday Independent*, but this time with an apology to Séamus, "not because I have to, but because I want to". He re-affirmed that his apology was not on foot of any legal, editorial, management or political threat, that it was "my decision and mine alone" and that it was "the decent thing to do". Explaining how the story came about, he said:

> Journalists know things only because people tip them off. And people who do rarely have altruistic motives. Great newspaper stories do not emerge from tribunals of inquiry. What level of proof then is required of a journalist? Editors and journalists will differ on that question. I tried to stand up the story, because that is what I am supposed to do. I thought I had stood it up. Then it sat down again. I am satisfied that Séamus Brennan's reputation remains intact. I say to him that I am sorry for putting him through this.

But it was not the journalists that Séamus blamed for the smears. He knew they were only doing their job. If blame was to be apportioned, it was reflected in the reasons why the person or persons ultimately responsible went to such evil extremes. Sigmund Freud, the father of psychoanalysis, said that "evil was something rooted in the person's past life". It could be a traumatic experience or a suppression of an emotion (most often anger) which influences a person's day-to-day life which may explode all of a sudden into blind rage. From Freud's perspective, evil was not a person. And it was this reasoning that allowed Séamus to successfully move on from those events.

Some six years later, Mairead Carey in the *Irish Voice* newspaper quoted former Attorney General, Progressive Democrat leader and minister, Michael McDowell, as saying that some elements within Fianna Fáil were "cowardly", "ruthless", "underhand", "resurgent" and "dangerous". She said that a spokesman for McDowell clarified that he was talking about a small group of Fianna Fáil people who had tried to destroy Séamus's career in 2002.

Shortly before Christmas 2002, *The Irish Times* published a tongue-in-cheek article by Killian Doyle which was headed "A Letter to Santa" which brought broad smiles to Séamus and his colleagues after what had been a turbulent few weeks:

Dear Santa,

I hope you and Mrs. Santa and all the elves are well and not too hassled about Christmas. I've been very good this year. You'd be very proud of me. Some bold boys tried to get me in trouble saying I'd been off smoking and drinking, but they're just jealous cos I got a new bigshot job, with a new office and loads of people to order around. It's much better than the old one where I had to nag people all day and get moaned at by Bertie when they didn't do what he wanted.

Listen, Santy. Don't believe Bertie when he tells you he's been good. He's probably got someone else to write his letter anyway. And don't give him any toys, he's already got loads of stuff. His mate, Charlie Mac is always taking our dinner money and buying things for him. You should give Charlie a lump of coal. Actually, don't – he'd probably just sell it.

My new office is deadly. There was a bit of yucky old lady at first, but that's long gone now. There were footprints on the desk too. I reckon the person who was there before had their feet up a lot.

I've made a huge big playroom out of one of the empty rooms in my building. It said "Dublin Metro System" on the door, but it was completely empty. Looks like nobody had ever gone in. Anyway, I've set up my train set and car racing track on a big table. I've even built a big tunnel for the trains to go through, and they come out the other end of the office where I've put all the model planes. There's a few other bits of track around but I haven't got enough for a full set. I just have to pretend for the moment.

I've got loads of little plastic people that I put on the trains. Sometimes I shove them all in at the same time for a laugh. It's funny seeing all their squidgy faces up against the glass. I put them on the platform sometimes and whizz the empty trains past them too. I like putting them beside the racetrack so I can zoom buses past and pour water on them at the same time. I know it's a bit mean, but it's not real, is it?

The lady who does all the real work asked me the other day why I put nearly everything over on one side of the room. I hadn't noticed, but she said I was ignoring the rest of the people in the other corners, and they'd get annoyed. She's mental! They're not even real people over there. I dunno why she got in such a huff. I think she's from Leitrim or Cavan or somewhere mad like that where they all drive around in tractors. But then I remembered that she makes my tea, so I chucked a few broken old cars and bits of bendy track around the room to keep her happy.

All the people who used to ask me horrible questions before are being nice and writing nice things about me. I think it's because I promised them I'd do loads of cool stuff next year and even let everyone have a go of the train set.

But then Charlie Mac told me off and took my toys off me. He said I won't get them back for years because the tiger had run off with them. I said there's no tigers in Ireland but he just shook his head and walked off, muttering something about paying me back in tacks.

So that's where you come in, Santa. I really, really need loads of new trains and carriages and buses and tracks and roads and other stuff so all the people I promised could play with them will still be my friends. Otherwise, me and Bertie and Charlie will have to go off and get real jobs.

Lots of love,

Séamus.

It is always nice to have a little bit of light relief – and this piece was something which Séamus got a great chuckle out of, seeing it as complementary to his own great wit. It perked him up and allowed him to forget the trauma of the previous few weeks.

Not one to remain in negative mode, Séamus next turned his attention to taxis as an integral part of the public transport system. Since Bobby Molloy, as Minister for the Environment, had deregulated taxis in November 2000, there had been ongoing clashes over the issue between the taxi industry, Opposition politicians, the Government, consumers and political commentators. For the taxi industry, the problem was that there were too many taxis which they felt corresponded with less work to share among the cartel of drivers; while consumers had long complained about long queues to get a taxi, particularly at peak times. Séamus agreed with the consumers and believed that the taxi unions wanted to keep taxi numbers down so as to keep the queues forming which they perceived as being good for business. But as always, wearing his economic hat, he believed in creating a stronger market which would itself bring more business and better standards.

With deregulation came a whole new way of dealing with the provision of public transport by taxi, and Séamus was determined to move quickly to consolidate the new arrangements. He wanted to do away with what he called "taxi drivers wearing string vests and driving clapped up cars in their spare time". He believed that the taxi industry needed to be staffed by full-time drivers who saw it as a real career, a point which was actually endorsed by the taxi unions. The first rung of this policy was the establishment of a Taxi Advisory Council, headed by former Garda Commissioner Pat Byrne, on 4 November 2003 (see Appendix 2 for a full list of membership). Three months later, on 14 February 2004, Séamus witnessed another development in his personal goals when an Interim Taxi Regulator, Jimmy Farrelly (former Secretary General, Department of the Environment and Local Government) took up his post on a temporary basis pending the necessary legislation. On July 26 that year, the country's first National Taxi Regulator, Ger Deering, was appointed, charged with setting standards for drivers and vehicles, including dress codes and a uniform colour for taxis. Making the announcement, Séamus said, "It offers the opportunity to foster a Cab Culture in Ireland similar to that in cities like London and New York".

He had succeeded in his personal challenge to officially integrate taxis and hackneys as part of the public transport fleet. However, one of the major issues which was not resolved was the uniform vehicle colour which Séamus told me was down squarely to the intransigence and blocking of the taxi unions despite Government commitments to financially assist full-time drivers, in much the same way as help was given to provide more wheelchair accessible taxis. A great opportunity to modernise the taxi fleet was temporarily lost, but it is inevitable that it will happen some day when there is another strong Minister for Transport in place.

One of Séamus's proudest moments was on 14 April 2004 when he had the opportunity as chairman of the EU Council of Transport Ministers to address the United Nations in New York. He used the occasion to call for the creation of a global road safety agency similar to the World Health Organisation to devise ways to reduce the number of road deaths worldwide. His idea was that:

> ... the proposed agency would monitor developments and trends in individual countries with a view to formulating future policies. An estimated 1.2 million people die in road accidents throughout the world annually and a further 50 million are injured each year.

But, as often happens with huge bureaucracies, this idea was put into international gestation but seemed to be a still birth.

One of his most significant achievements during the second time in Transport, and the one for which he will forever be remembered, was the roll out of the Luas light rail system in June 2004 (which you will recall began life many years before as Séamus's wish to re-open the Harcourt Street to Bray rail line). The success of the Luas completion was all the more remarkable when it was discovered that the Minister for Finance, Charlie McCreevy, had written to the Taoiseach in the summer of 2001 (while Mary O'Rourke was minister) expressing "strong reservations", but there was no way that it was going to be delayed while Séamus Brennan was in the hot seat. He was not going to be a party to any loss of public confidence in the political commitment which had been given to the early delivery of public transport projects as a key election manifesto commitment. Nor was he going to give up on what was a key personal project.

His usual indomitable spirit was brought to bear and the fight back began. His strong case was accepted by the Minister for Finance and the Government. While Charlie McCreevy was the approving Finance Minister, it was since speculated that had his successor, Brian Cowen (who had mothballed the Harcourt Street Line project when he succeeded Séamus as Transport Minister 12 years earlier), been Finance Minister at the time, it might have been a more difficult fight. It is amazing how things go full circle in political life.

The Green Line from Sandyford to St. Stephen's Green was the first to be opened in June 2004 ahead of schedule. It had a particular resonance for Séamus due to his earlier work at the foundation of this project.

But it was also a significant political feat for Séamus as for years he had to listen to Opposition politicians and others saying that it would never happen. The proof of the pudding was in the eating and those who did not have the opportunity, the energy, the drive or the commitment to work at the project were forced to eat substantial humble pie.

The point was further stressed when two months later, Séamus asked Taoiseach Bertie Ahern if he would do the honours in opening the Red Line from Tallaght to Connolly Station, which included a piece of the Taoiseach's own constituency of Dublin Central.

From a competition perspective, it was important that this new system would be operated by a private company under a contract of service rather than letting the national transport company, CIÉ, run it. The key to its success was, and is, reliability. Within a very short period, it was already operating ahead of projected passenger numbers and was making a profit when the capital cost was taken out.

One of the things that Séamus learned from his previous stint in Transport was the difficulty in properly planning infrastructural projects when funding was only allocated on a year-to-year basis, and this was brought home by the lengthy delay in getting the Luas up and running and the slowness of road infrastructure projects. He was therefore determined to press for multi-annual funding for major transport projects, particularly the inter-city motorway system which had been plodding along in bits and pieces.

Drawing up a strong case, he went to see the Minister for Finance, Charlie McCreevy. Dogged negotiator that Séamus was, he was not going to leave McCreevy's office without managing to secure an agreement for the required multi-annual funding. He got his wish for €7 billion over three years for an accelerated national roads programme in what was a first for budgetary frameworks, and this allowed major road projects to proceed at a far faster and more efficient way than previously. The agreement also paved the

way for Séamus to instruct the National Roads Authority to put in
fixed price contracts which transformed the roads programme as
such contracts were invariably completed ahead of schedule, providing much better value for the taxpayer.

Other important achievements in Transport included securing
extra funding to complete a study on re-opening the Western Rail
Corridor (which later led to the physical building work beginning),
and what subsequently became the Garda Traffic Corps. The latter
item had been the subject of intensive consultations between the
Department of Transport, the Department of Justice (under Minister Michael McDowell) and senior gardaí. Séamus had a vision of
a specially formed Traffic Corps which would concentrate on en-
forcing road traffic law and he publicly committed to do this under
his own Department if the Department of Justice and the gardai
were not open to it.

The plan to set up a Traffic Corps through his own Department
was Séamus's master stroke because it had the effect of galvanis-
ing others who did not want to see the role of the Garda Siochána
usurped in traffic matters. In truth, Séamus did not want to have
responsibility for a Traffic Corps because he also did not want to
dilute the Garda Siochána. "The goal was the important thing, not
the manner in which it was achieved," he said to me privately. And
so resources were found by Minister McDowell that allowed the
Garda Traffic Corps to be born with its own branded Garda vehicles and personnel.

The success Séamus had with the Traffic Corps was acknowledged by Killian Doyle in *The Irish Times*:

> He showed that what he lacked in stature, he made up
> for in mettle when he set the Traffic Corps ball rolling,
> despite having to shove it up the mountain of resistance
> from Darth McDowell, Chuckles McCreevy and the
> Phoenix Park Garda honchos.

However, it was the steering through of legislation to introduce
penalty points (they came into force on 31 October 2002) that
showed again that Séamus would not bow down to excuses from

any source. He always said that he was "not interested in excuses, only solutions". In a statement issued the day before their introduction, he said, "The ultimate goal is to bring about a radical change in driver behaviour".

To have achieved such a major shift in road policy was quite remarkable at a time when it seemed there was what Martha Kearns in the *Irish Independent* of 29 October 2002 called "a virtual revolt by Gardaí". The Association of Garda Sergeants and Inspectors had dismissed the introduction of penalty points as "excessively bureaucratic and a waste of resources", while the Garda Representative Association had said it was "ham-fisted, unprofessional and unworkable". Séamus had heard these sort of views expressed at several meetings involving Garda personnel who complained that they had no appropriate computer system in place, but he knew in his heart and soul that lives could not wait for the Gardaí to be ready – he had to call their bluff and do what was the right thing to do. After all, penalty points were not a new invention – their introduction elsewhere resulted in a dramatic downward effect on road fatalities when combined with effective enforcement.

His compromise was to introduce penalty points on a phased basis being handled manually by Gardaí, with the important computer linkage to the National Driver File being outsourced to a company in Cork. He would not countenance any delay to the principle any longer, particularly as penalty points had been first promised in 1997 at the launch of a five-year road safety strategy by then Environment Minister, Bobby Molloy.

The first offence to carry penalty points was speeding. In his statement, Séamus said:

> Excessive speed is recognised as the most significant contribution to road accidents. The simple fact is that speed kills and maims a great many people every year. It must be curtailed if we are to make the roads safer for all drivers.

While he never agreed that there was an acceptable figure for the number of road deaths, he was glad to see that in the first year after the introduction of penalty points the number of annual road deaths fell below 400 for the first time in 17 years.

But even with that dramatic drop, Séamus was still cautious. In an interview with Eoghan Williams in the *Sunday Independent*, he said that "what we are really about is not catching people, we're about changing the driving culture".

The statistical reduction in road deaths was widely attributed to the introduction of penalty points and remains as a testament to the vision of a truly reforming Minister. Writing in *The Irish Times* on 13 December 2002, Miriam Donohoe said:

> Criticism is heaped often enough by commentators on politicians who don't deliver on their promises, and rightly so. But in the case of our Minister for Transport, congratulations are in order. I don't know if his colleagues around the Cabinet table are patting him on the back for his initiative, but the lesson for all politicians would appear to be this: be your own person and don't let reluctant lobby groups and civil servants and public servants stand in the way of a major decision if you believe it makes a lot of sense and is for the common good.

His fame as the Penalty Points Minister even reached *The New York Times* when an article by Brian Lavery was published on Christmas Eve, 2002 which praised the "aggressive Government Minister" who brought in penalty points "against the police force's objections about too much paperwork and inadequate computer systems".

At the end of 2002, Treacy Hogan wrote in the *Irish Independent* that the introduction of penalty points showed that "for a small man, he can pack a mighty punch". Or, as Eoghan Williams in the *Sunday Independent* said, "Admirers of Brennan's say it is not the policies which are radical, but the fact that the Minister is implementing them".

The "culture change" which Séamus endorsed was born out of a real life situation from the Millennium Year, 2000, when he lost his only sister's husband, John Forde, in a car crash on the road between Shannon and Galway. Talking to Eoghan Williams in the *Sunday Independent* about the crash for the first time, he had revealed that it was his brother-in-law's birthday and 11.00 in the morning: "A guy in a truck, who the Court subsequently found was drinking Benelyn, came across the road. It killed him stone dead."

However, a few months after the introduction of penalty points, some Gardaí still appeared to be smarting over effectively being forced to apply the points by manual methods. A confidential report by the Internal Audit Section at Garda Headquarters, which was mentioned on the floor of Dáil Éireann, made the startling claim that "the system is on the verge of collapse", that Gardaí do not have sufficient resources to operate the system and that a backlog has built up that may lead to offenders escaping penalties". In a strong defence , Séamus gave an interview to RTÉ radio in which he repeated that there was absolutely no reason why the Gardaí could not press ahead using the resources they had been allocated.

And in a pointed barb at the Gardaí, he noted his "surprise that they had found time to conduct an audit on the system only two or three months after its introduction". He also expressed surprise "at the speed with which the report found its way into the public arena". He was adamant that the system was working and would continue to work. That straight talking had the effect of cooling the situation – at least in public – but there was no doubt that some members of the Guardians of the Peace remained upset at the effect of having to use manual means to implement the law in the short term.

As a former commerce graduate of both University College Galway and University College Dublin, Séamus was intrigued to find that the *Irish Independent* story about the "virtual revolt" of the Gardaí, and his handling of the penalty points issue, was the subject of examination questions for students of the B.Comm at the National University of Ireland, Galway in 2003, when the examiners posed the following questions for their students:

> What problem is the Transport Minister attempting to solve? Is this a 'difficulty' or a 'mess'? Is the approach taken by the Minister to implement change 'hard' or 'soft'? Was the approach appropriate given the nature of the problem?

An analysis of the answers would be an interesting exercise.

Allied to penalty points, Séamus was also keen to end the cavalier attitude many people seemed to have with driving licences, and to end the situation where hundreds of thousands of drivers did not have full licences. At the time, one in six Irish drivers – 325,000 people – never passed a driving test and many of those people had provisional licences for up to two decades. Statistics showed that they were 50 times more likely to get into accidents than those who passed the test.

He wanted 2003 to be "the year the holding of a driving licence becomes a privilege, not a right". But part of the solution involved identifying more testers and getting existing testers to do more tests. It suited the existing testers to have long queues as it meant constant work for them and, in turn, more overtime, and they did their best to ensure that the status quo would remain.

But Séamus was determined to honour his pledge to overhaul the system, particularly what he described as a "silly anomaly" – the loophole that allowed people who have failed their second driving test to receive another provisional licence immediately and to drive away from the test centre by themselves. After much discussion and threats of industrial action, Séamus got Government approval to outsource up to 10,000 tests and agreement that the existing testers would work late in the summer months and at weekends. This led to Conor Faughnan of the Automobile Association saying:

> There is evidence that we're beginning to take road safety seriously in this country. It's certainly very high on the political agenda.

At some time in 2003, Séamus discovered that his own driving licence was out of date – he had no need of one for many years due to his ministerial roles. But it was not simply a matter of applying, even for a minister – the rules required that a person with an out of date licence had to re-sit the driving test, and do the new theory test. Séamus got his Road Safety Booklet to study, applied for a theory test, took the test the same as every other learner and subsequently passed.

The challenge now was to pass the actual driving test in the same way as every other applicant. And so the formal application was sent in. As he had not driven for some time, he wanted to arrange some lessons to be sure that he was up to speed as it were, if you will pardon the pun. When Séamus asked the question about who he could get to teach him without drawing too much attention to himself, this author recommended former rally driver Rosemary Smith, who was also a constituent, and who had successfully taught the author's daughter some years previously. Contact was made and Rosemary agreed to take Séamus as a learner. Proving himself still adept at driving, which he had of course done for many years prior to becoming a minister, he was deemed ready for the test after just a few lessons and in the normal way a test date was given.

On the day of the test, Séamus went along to the local test centre in Rathgar and, using Rosemary's car, he passed with flying colours – another notch for Rosemary Smith. Indeed, it would have been somewhat unfortunate if the serving Minister for Transport had failed, but he got no special treatment, nor did he want any. As far as he was concerned, he wanted to be the same as any other nervous learner going to the test centre.

Returning to the speeding issue, preparations were well in hand for the biggest logistical operation in the history of the country – the changeover from miles to kilometres – which was set to take place on 1 January 2005. Some 58,000 new road signs are believed to have been produced and were erected in the months before with plastic coverings to avoid confusing road users. Séamus had asked that speed limits be reviewed in tandem with this exercise, before signs were produced, to ensure they were appropriate. He believed that inappropriate speed limits would not be respected, whereas if those using the roads believed a speed limit was suitable there would be much greater adherence to it. He always used the example of the Stillorgan dual carriageway which, as a three lane road on each side, had a lower speed limit (50 kilometres per hour) than many "boreens" around the country which had 80 kilometres per hour limits. This view was shared by RTÉ's Pat Kenny who gave airtime to the grievance about this particular stretch of road. But this was one request which was not granted – and indeed, almost as if he was being snubbed, there were suggestions later that the limit might go even lower than 50 kilometres per hour.

Among the most difficult issues which Séamus faced in any Department was getting to grips with breaking down the monopolies in aviation and public transport. Shane Ross in the *Sunday Independent* called him "an instinctive champion of enterprise", and from past events, he knew that vintage vested interests were at play locally and nationally which did not want to see any change taking place. But this just galvanised Séamus into stronger action which he believed was in the interests of the consumer.

The aviation world was expanding, even as it came out of the tragic events of 11 September 2001 in the USA. Aer Lingus had negotiated a survival plan, while Ryanair had become known as Ireland's second "national" airline. Aer Arran was growing steadily and City Jet was offering a number of important services. The time was right for the three State airports – Dublin, Cork and Shannon – to become separate State companies with their own boards and to compete with each other for services from both domestic and international airlines. Shane Ross, writing in the *Sunday Independent*, said:

> The very word 'competition' is heresy out at Dublin Airport. Separate companies means separate boards. Separate boards means loss of office for some.

The airport operating authority was the State owned Aer Rianta which was responsible for the three State airports and was based at Dublin Airport. At the same time, a number of private provincial airports were working away without the constraints of being tied to Aer Rianta and were achieving good returns on their investments. Even Knock Airport (which had been laughed at when first conceived by Monsignor Horan in the early 1980s) was in the black.

Séamus wanted the airports to be run like commercial businesses and that meant securing experienced board members who understood business, whether they were political supporters of the Government or not. The skill he wanted for board appointments was the ability to do the necessary job, regardless of political allegiance – and if that meant that some political supporters would have to step aside, or stay out of the equation, then so be it. This was a new departure as politicians of all shades had previously seen appointments to the boards of major semi-state bodies as rewards for political support, whether those appointed had the necessary expertise or not.

As expected, some of the board of Aer Rianta were at one with the trade unions in being opposed to any change to the status quo. It would upset their cosy little arrangement as there would be no room for them on the new boards. In this view, they were also at one with Sinn Féin, whose Spokesperson on Transport, Sean Crowe TD, had issued a public call for the proposals to be scrapped – a call which was never going to be heeded.

But in order to keep an eye on all sides in the debate, and to have some insider knowledge, Séamus asked this author to liaise confidentially with two friendly trade union sources to get their views on the developments, and to then report back to him alone. Several private meetings were held at secret locations and the intelligence passed and received was extraordinarily helpful as the reform plans were progressing.

Having discussed his ideas with Taoiseach Bertie Ahern, Séamus understood that he had full support to move forward with radical proposals to tackle the outdated practices which he believed permeated the aviation and public transport sectors.

During the passage of the legislation through the Seanad, opposition to it had come from a most unlikely source – the former Minister Mary O'Rourke, who was then Leader of the Seanad, having been appointed as one of the Taoiseach's nominees. Mary was known as "Mammy" to her peers in Leinster House because of her habit of appearing to be an old fashioned school mistress in talking down to them. She seemed to find it difficult to reconcile the treble loss of her seat in Westmeath at the general election (to her arch rival, Donie Cassidy), the consequential loss of her ministry, and the loss of the Deputy Leadership of Fianna Fáil .

In an interview attributed to her in *Hot Press* magazine and quoted by Mary Minihan in *The Irish Times*, "Mammy" told the story of how she became Leader of the Seanad. Recounting how "she really stood up" to then Taoiseach, Bertie Ahern, she told of how she demanded both a Taoiseach's nomination and the post of Leader because she believed that the election strategy put in place by Fianna Fáil had been the cause of her losing the general election and the two spin-off effects. When she was re-elected to the Dáil five years later in 2007, she changed places with her rival Donie Cassidy in two unique ways: she regained what she viewed as her Dáil seat from Cassidy, and he was appointed to her former post as Leader of Seanad Éireann (a post he had also filled from 1997 to 2002).

But it was on the State Airports Bill that "Mammy" did what can only be described as "some strange things" to Séamus Brennan as her ministerial successor. She consistently and publicly supported a Fine Gael claim that the Bill was flawed, that it was "rushed, premature and not good legislation" because it had been drafted by a private firm of solicitors, Matheson Ormsby Prentice, rather than by the Parliamentary Draftsman's Office. The reason for using outside drafting expertise was due to what Séamus said would have been "an unacceptable delay" in getting the necessary legislation into force because of a backlog in the Parliamentary Draftsman's Office.

During the debate in the Seanad, tough words were exchanged between the two Fianna Fáil heavyweights. Séamus was as ever the conciliator, but he found it increasingly hard to bite his tongue, saying:

> The Leader of the House was entitled to disagree with me and she did. I am entitled to disagree with that direction. I do not support that policy of my predecessor. She is fully entitled to take me to task about my policy. I am fully entitled to respond and say I do not like her direction.

In the same debate, Senator Fergal Browne, Fine Gael Spokesman on Transport, said:

> One wonders if Senator O'Rourke is the real Opposition spokesperson on Transport. Perhaps I have lost my role in that regard.

But in what was a remarkably quick turnaround from concept to Oireachtas approval, pioneering legislation (State Airports Act 2004) was passed which would see Aer Rianta abolished and the three airports having their own boards – Dublin Airport Authority, Cork Airport Authority and Shannon Airport Authority – with effect from 1 October 2004 (see Appendix 2 for full list of membership). When the Bill was about to be passed in the Dáil, the Labour Party Spokesman, Derek McDowell, thanked Mary O'Rourke for what he said was the "sterling leadership" she gave to the Opposition.

No amount of clarification from either Séamus or the Attorney-General satisfied the woman who had been minister, who was rejected by her own electorate, and who was not elected to the Seanad. For any Leader of the Seanad to adopt such a strong public position in opposition to a senior Fianna Fáil colleague was akin to GUBU ("grotesque, unbelievable, bizarre, unprecedented" – the words used by Charlie Haughey in previous years regarding other strange matters). Yet no public sanction was applied to her by the Taoiseach or Fianna Fáil, something which would not have been tolerated if such a lack of discipline was displayed by a lesser fig-ure. Indeed, people had been expelled from the Fianna Fáil Par-liamentary Party for much more minor reasons in the past. Here again was a sign that Bertie Ahern may have wanted to be seen to appease his trade union friends regardless of the cost.

It is hardly surprising that this period marked a significant de-terioration in the normal political comradeship between Séamus Brennan and Mary O'Rourke as two members of the same party, a rift which never really healed.

Frank Fitzgibbon in *The Sunday Times* noted that what he called "the modest proposals to split the airport operator into three independent units" was a step too far for the "neanderthal tendencies" of trade union leaders, before going on to write that "the saga of the Aer Rianta breakup confirms there is no talking to the belligerent activists who will use their own narrow agenda to destroy the image of the country as a whole".

Although the outgoing Chairman of Aer Rianta, Noel Hanlon, had been described in the *Donegal Times* on 11 December 2002 as "political adviser and friend to Albert Reynolds (former Tao-iseach) for over thirty years", Séamus and the department had a tempestuous relationship with him. Hanlon spectacularly diverted from normal protocol by siding with the trade unions in being publicly critical of the legislation being proposed by his political superior, even going so far as to describe it as "draconian" in an exclusive interview with RTÉ News on 23 June 2004. He and the trade unions believed it was a step towards privatisation, a famil-iar argument put forward by the trade union movement whenever Séamus brought forward proposals to reform public services, even though there was simply no mechanism within the State Airports Act for privatisation to apply.

In fact, Séamus strongly supported the idea of the three State airports continuing to be owned by the State in much the same way as the road network and train tracks are owned by the State. He would not countenance any privatisation of the State airports, but did want them to be in a position to compete with each other as independent State entities.

It was highly unusual for a serving chairman of a semi-state body to adopt such an aggressive public stance; and more unusual again because of Hanlon's past clashes with trade unions when he closed what seemed to be a very profitable ambulance manufacturing plant in Longford rather than give in to trade union demands at the time. But as the online edition of *The Sunday Business Post* (ThePost.ie) had said four years previously:

> Hanlon's obduracy is his hallmark. His opponents label
> him a union buster but his stubbornness is a sign of grit
> to his admirers.

Whatever chance Hanlon had of continuing his long career as a ministerial nominee at different times on various boards (Foir Teoranta, VHI, Aer Lingus, and then Aer Rianta), there was now "no way in the wide earthly world" (as the Kerry TD, Jackie Healy-Rae, would say about many things) that Séamus would tolerate any further insubordination from a semi-state chairman. Hanlon's strident criticism of the reform plans signalled the end of any form of working relationship and, as a result, the end of Hanlon's career in public bodies.

The question was whether Hanlon would be allowed to continue as chairman until the end of his term, which coincided with the effective date for the new legislation. There was certainly a strong view that he should be immediately sacked, but this was tempered by not wanting him to have the opportunity to be seen as a sacrificial lamb, and the latter view prevailed. Hanlon continued to serve out the remaining months of his term without any sign of contrition and continued to have intermittent spats with his minister and the Department of Transport over a variety of issues, including a controversial termination payment to the Aer Rianta Chief Executive, Margaret Sweeney, who had been in the job for just six months (although she had been Assistant Chief Executive before that). In some ways, she could be viewed as the unwitting pawn of Hanlon as he saw out his final days as chairman, although there is a suggestion that she had been unable to get clarification of what her role would be when the new Dublin Airport Authority took over. Séamus was annoyed that neither Hanlon nor Sweeney seemed to grasp the clear fact that her role was a matter for the new semi-state Dublin Airport Authority and who they wanted as Chief Executive, not a matter for the department or the minister.

The *Irish Independent* would later claim that there had been "an almost complete collapse in relations between all the major parties involved in the break-up of the airport authority". In an article headed "Bitter Aer Rianta break-up exposed" on 14 November 2004, the paper quoted extensively from letters exchanged between the Secretary-General of the Department and the Chairman of Aer Rianta which explicitly stated that "the appointment and the proposed exit terms (of Sweeney) are unacceptable to the Department". Even more strongly worded was the bold statement that the proposed payment "would be unlawful and would constitute a most serious breach of fiduciary duty on behalf of the Board generally and on the part of each individual Board Member to the shareholder". As if to amplify that strong language, the correspondence said that the termination payment was "so extraordinary and so commercially reckless that the mere entering into such agreement by the Board was in breach of the Board's duty".

However, despite the strong language and the legal doubts on the exit terms for Margaret Sweeney, the payment of a six to seven figure sum was eventually approved by the new Authority which did not want the hassle of a protracted legal case.

Away from these administrative matters between the department and Aer Rianta, Séamus had pondered at very considerable length and consulted with a tight circle of close advisers about the right composition for the new boards, as he did with any board appointments which were made during his long ministerial life. He wanted the airport boards to be made up of aviation and business experts tempered by other appropriate skill sets, and four positions on each board were reserved for worker–directors to ensure that any union concerns would have the opportunity to be properly aired. But as the trade unions remained in dispute about the legislation, they would not take up their posts at the same time as the other appointments.

To allow time for technical issues to be worked out, full autonomy for Shannon and Cork was to be deferred for a period while the ownership of assets at all three airports was resolved. While the old regime of Aer Rianta had ensured that Dublin Airport remained the dominant body, with the two other airports being indebted to Dublin in a financial sense, there was an interim compromise with a sting: each airport would be responsible for its own marketing and negotiating with airlines – but for a time, their plans would be subject to being approved by the Dublin Airport Authority as the successor of Aer Rianta.

For the present, the chairs of Cork and Shannon would be ex-officio on the board of Dublin Airport Authority, but as soon as the transfer of assets took place, the three airports would be deemed to be self-sufficient and would operate without cross representation on boards. As Cork Airport had already embarked on the construction of a new terminal under Aer Rianta, it was also intended that an independent Cork Airport Authority would be given a clean slate and would not have to bear the cost of the new terminal in their independent guise.

It was quite ironic – or maybe even deliberate – that just two days before the abolition of Aer Rianta and the realisation of one of Séamus's great reforms, Bertie Ahern decided to reshuffle his cabinet and, in the process, take Séamus out of the picture. It was well known that Bertie was close to the trade union movement which may have sometimes muddied necessary reforms in the public sector. Jim McGuire, writing in the *Western People* said:

> When it came to a choice between shafting Brennan who had been openly dedicated to reform in road and air transport, or appeasing the trade unions in designated power positions, Bertie chose (as he always has) to keep the comrades happy if not by another spate of benchmarking than by pulling the thorn Brennan from the paws of the bigger cats.

There was no doubt that Séamus's work as Minister for Transport was like a festering sore as far as the trade unions were concerned – he was getting too close to upsetting their "cosy cartel" with his strong instinct for reforms – and they piled the pressure on their chief supporter in Government, one Bertie Ahern. The newly found friend of the trade unions, Noel Hanlon, in his last hours as Chairman of Aer Rianta, could not resist a final swipe when he said on RTÉ that it was "a great relief to aviation interests that Séamus Brennan has been transferred from the Department of Transport". But it remains unclear on whose behalf he was speaking because other significant "aviation interests" were severely critical of the removal of Séamus from Transport.

There were also many who were appalled that vested interests appeared to have such sway with the leader of the country. That influence went back to Ahern's days as Minister for Labour in the late 1980s when he was known as a one-man strike fixer, a period described by John Downing in some detail in his book *Most Skilful, Most Devious, Most Cunning*.

A potentially explosive situation erupted in the Dáil the following month when the then Labour Party Leader, Pat Rabbitte was involved in a heated debate during which he made controversial remarks which appeared to imply that Séamus had received "inducements" from Michael O'Leary, Chief Executive of Ryanair, in regard to the breakup of Aer Rianta into three separate companies. But Rabbitte withdrew the comments the following day insisting his remarks were misinterpreted and that he "did not intend to suggest that the Minister had received inducements from Mr. O'Leary". As the remarks were made under Dáil privilege, there was no legal remedy open to Séamus for what could otherwise have been a case of slander.

With aviation now notched up, Séamus again set his sights on the CIÉ group, which he saw as the next semi-state sector in need of major reform.

On a parallel track to addressing the Aer Rianta breakup, Séamus wanted to open up the Dublin bus market so that private operators could compete effectively with the State operator, Bus

Atha Cliath, while at the same time enhancing and upgrading the State service. He was encouraged in this thinking by the success of a number of private operators who had secured limited licences, principally on the long haul routes in competition with Bus Éire-ann, but also on routes such as Dublin City to Dublin Airport and some services from the Dublin suburbs to the city centre.

On 29 July 2002, shortly after taking up office in Transport, Séamus issued a statement which clearly set out the path he was going to follow, a path which he had been trying to go down since the time he was Minister for Transport ten years earlier:

> While acknowledging the valuable contribution of CIÉ's dedicated management and staff, I feel it is now time to take stock of the adequacies of our transport system, of its ability to meet future demands and challenges, and of CIÉ's central and future role in the provision of such a transport system. The losses recorded by CIÉ, which indicate deterioration in the overall financial position despite a significant increase in State support for the provision of public services, are extremely disappointing and are a matter of serious concern to the Government.
>
> These are issues that require urgent attention and I intend to address the need for changes over the coming months in the context of an overall institutional and regulatory organisation of the public transport system.

Séamus indicated that he was looking at allowing private op-erators to apply for licences to operate services in 25 per cent of the bus market in Dublin. The immediate effect of this policy di-rection was seen in two divergent ways: predictable trade union opposition combined with Bus Atha Cliath becoming more pro-active in identifying new routes – but also appearing to be pro-active in using their muscle to inhibit private operators from ap-plying for licences, a charge which Bus Atha Cliath and CIÉ have always denied.

While there were supporters of the new proposals within man-agement, there were also some who did not want to give way. In this stance, the trade unions and some of the management were at one – something which they had in common with Aer Rianta but which was not often the case for the CIÉ companies which had been dogged over the years by regular industrial disputes, both official and unofficial, in what were sometimes termed "lightening strikes" (as if that terminology somehow made them ok), which in turn led to severe inconvenience for the travelling public and a further loss of confidence in publicly operated transport. The attitude of the trade unions seemed to be that the taxpayer would just pick up the slack when the CIÉ companies balance sheet was down. It was this mentality that Séamus wanted to confront as it had not been challenged by any of his successors since his first stint as Minister for Transport between 1989 and 1992.

The British-based Transport Salaried Staffs' Association (TSAA) got in on the opposition to the plans, probably because their former Irish Secretary, Gerry Doherty, was now based in London as their Development Manager. But as usual, the trade union seemed to get the wrong end of the stick when it was claimed that the proposals amounted to privatisation of public transport. As with Aer Rianta, this was not on Séamus's agenda – he knew there would always be a need for State-run public transport. What he wanted to do was to make the State-run bodies more efficient at what they did, not to sell off a national asset.

Séamus saw this as typical trade union opposition to any proposal for doing things in a better way, and the real reason behind it was laid bare in the TSAA statement:

> The dramatic fall in bus drivers' pay package after privatisation (in Britain) has led to a crisis in recruitment and retention of frontline staff. It's reasonable to suppose that this experience will be replicated in Ireland, so instead of creating jobs, as Séamus Brennan suggests when 25% of Dublin Bus is hived off, we predict the opposite. Inexperience and staff shortages have resulted in a failure to deliver adequate bus services, short changing customers who have no alternative to the bus.

This was rightly seen by Séamus as "nonsense", and in later years was proven very effectively with the Luas which has been operated privately from the beginning (and profitably from an early stage) despite competition for the travelling public from Dublin Bus. What the trade union really meant was that the secure status of public service employment, with all the benefits that went with that, would obviously not apply to private operators. Drivers would therefore have to be more commercially minded, something which was unlikely to happen within a cushioned State monopoly.

But then, even the political voice of the trade unions was not always speaking the same language. The ultra left wing Socialist Party clashed with the main CIÉ trade unions, SIPTU and the NBRU, accusing them of caving in and "forcing the workers in CIÉ and Aer Rianta, against their wishes" to pull back from threatened strikes on the basis of Government assurances from the old friend of the unions, Bertie Ahern, when they were told that the proposals would "protect current jobs". As they were being snubbed, the Socialist Party tried a last ditch effort to drum up support using four points in uncompromising language:

1. Don't accept any deal that will sell-off the future jobs and conditions of bus workers.

2. Competition means profiteering and privatisation by stealth – no franchising of any routes.

3. Organise for a 24 hour strike action to derail the plans of the Government and union leaders.

4. Work for a properly funded and modern public transport system with affordable fares.

But Séamus wanted to go further and break up the monolith which CIÉ had become, and the union language only spurred him on.

He wanted to see Bus Atha Cliath, Iarnrod Éireann and Bus Éireann become independent State companies with the CIÉ holding company abolished in a similar way to the reforms at Dublin, Cork and Shannon Airports. It appeared to him that CIÉ, as a corporate body, had no real commercial function and that the three companies would be better able for the reality of commercial life by being given full responsibility, as semi-state companies, for their effective and efficient operations.

Following on from this, and at a time when Bus Atha Cliath was seeking funding for 500 extra buses, Séamus decided to do his own ad hoc survey of Dublin services. He recruited one of his brothers to go with him incognito to the city centre and quietly observed 92 buses only half full in the period around the 5.00 pm peak. That simple statistic would give him the ammunition to talk commercial reality figures with Dublin Bus.

On the surface, it appeared that Séamus again had the explicit approval of Taoiseach Bertie Ahern to pursue his major reform policy, as the Taoiseach had previously said publicly that "problems in public services cannot be solved unless working practices change", and all proposals had been run by the Taoiseach and the cabinet as a matter of course before they were publicly announced.

But some other agenda appeared to be simmering below the surface in Bertie Ahern's mind and would have reverberations into the future. The vision of support from the Taoiseach, which Séamus believed he had, was to be weakened considerably before too long.

Hours of intensive meetings were held at both official and Ministerial levels at which public transport unions heard directly of the reform plans. But as expected, they indicated that they were prepared to fight tooth and nail to try to prevent any opening up of the market. Mary Dundon in the *Irish Examiner*, quoting trade union leaders, wrote that commuters would face "massive rail and bus disruption" unless the proposed reforms to CIÉ were scrapped. This led to Séamus making a strident declaration in May 2003 in which he warned the travelling public that he expected "a summer of discontent". It was clear to Séamus that the CIÉ trade unions were once more trying to force the elected Government to back down on reform plans which had been openly displayed in the Programme for Government which was laid before the electorate, and on which the Government therefore had a mandate, and he was not prepared to go down that anti-democratic road just to appease them. Public transport had been crying out for reform for far too long and he felt a public duty and an obligation to take up from where he had left off in 1992. Despite Government talks with the Irish Congress of Trade Unions to try to defuse the situation, there was no successful outcome and the talks were considered to be only the usual "frank exchange of views".

Once again, Séamus was in the position where he had to stare down public transport trade unions whose members had been excessively cushioned from independent commercial life, given that CIÉ had always enjoyed significant State subsidies each year. He was appalled, but not surprised given his experience with them previously, that the transport unions were not prepared to let anyone muscle in on what they perceived to be their patch, and that they did not appear to be even prepared to discuss options for the future. The trade union attitude was epitomised by one of the leaders who was so radical that even other trade unions had problems with him – Brendan Ogle. In his book, *The Story of ILDA* (Irish Locomotive Drivers Association), he said that "Brennan is a 'dodo', he was one of Jack Lynch's whizz kids and he's a failed PD-er". But neither Ogle nor other trade unions had offered any alternative, preferring instead to continue the old mantra so beloved of trade union leaders – and at one time, beloved of certain politicians in the North of Ireland – "no surrender".

The parent company of the public transport operators, Córas Iompair Eireann (CIÉ), had seen its taxpayer's subsidy climb each year while many consumers felt that some of the services provided could more usefully be carried out by private commercial companies that would not require taxpayer funds. The private operators promised reliability of services, which was something not always achieved by the CIÉ companies at that time.

The public mood was for services which were available when they wanted them, and which represented good value together with a degree of comfort. The mechanism for responding to the public demand was a twin-pronged approach to inject capital into the CIÉ companies for new vehicles and to open up the market on the basis that if services were available, people would use them. The old policy of only providing services after an area was developed was no longer viable.

For the first six months of 2004, Ireland held the rotating Presidency of the European Union and, as Transport Minister, Séamus was President of the Transport Council of Ministers. He had the opportunity to address the Council on January 21 with the theme of "Europeans – Working Together", which he explained was intended to "capture a vision of the people of the European Union working as a team, striving together to achieve our ambitious common goals and objectives".

This was a glorious opportunity to return to one of his favourite topics – public transport – and to stitch some particular comments into the European record. He spoke of the "urgent need to make the railway sector, a key economic sector in the Union, more dynamic and competitive" and said that this could be done "through the opening-up of the railway freight market". And he also referred to "rail liberalisation". Now these comments, while having a resonance at home, were actually more related to the continent of Europe with its vast land frontiers, where transport of goods by rail was strategically important; but the important thing for Séamus was to have the issues on the European record as an adjunct to his own reform proposals in Ireland.

At a Council of Ministers meeting in Brussels two months later, one of the issues was a plan for money obtained from road tolls. In Euro-speak, the "Eurovignette" plan proposed by the Commission was to harmonise national toll and road charge systems for lorries using a "polluter-pays" principle where drivers would pay for the infrastructure they use. Séamus, as President, was in the chair and he had been hoping for a compromise deal. But after a day of talks, ministers remained deeply divided on a number of issues. The main problem was over the revenue from the road tolls which the Commission wanted Member States to re-invest in infrastructure to relieve bottlenecks and congestion.

However, a strong group of ministers from Germany, Britain, France, Belgium, Denmark, and Sweden – together with Ireland – were strongly opposed to this suggestion, feeling that giving in on this would open the way for the Commission to interfere in other financial matters. They wanted to retain the right to allocate financial resources in whatever way was appropriate to their own economies.

With such "divergent views", as Séamus said at the post-Council press conference, it was inevitable that agreement would not be reached under Ireland's Presidency. Who was it that said "patience is a virtue"? At any rate, Séamus well knew that it takes time to resolve multinational difficulties, and as it turned out 13 months later, the matter was resolved under the Presidency of Luxembourg in favour of the Irish view, which recalled to mind the old Irish proverb, "It is a long road that has no turning".

But it was the "long road that has no turning" which complicated his goal of disentangling the three public transport operating companies from the CIÉ monolith. His intention was to introduce a CIÉ Companies Bill which would be similar to the State Airports Act in that there would be three independent State companies (Bus Atha Cliath, Bus Éireann and Iarnrod Éireann) and the practise of having some common directors, including the chairman, among them would be ended. While he had set the ball in motion by not re-appointing board members whose terms had expired, it was time pressure – and Bertie Ahern's reshuffle of ministers – which meant that no other progress was made on that reform issue.

Later in the summer, Séamus was asked to represent the Government at an International Summit on Democracy, Terrorism and Security in Madrid, chaired by Martii Ahtisaari, Former President of Finland, who would later play a crucial role in the Northern Ireland Peace Process. This tested Séamus's abilities in new areas and it showed that even in the sensitive areas under discussion, he could be depended on to perform. During a wide ranging formal address, he noted that terrorism recognised no boundaries "whether they are geographic, religious or political", and that the aim of those involved in terrorism was "to create international instability".

In a direct reference to Northern Ireland, he noted that:

> ... we have had our share of terrorism on the island for many, many years and we've learned one thing: terrorism is a complex problem. We've learned that a solution to terrorism that's based exclusively on security considerations alone will not be effective.

Going on to endorse the work of the then Secretary General of the United Nations, Kofi Annan, he added the important rider that "condemnation is important, but condemnation alone is not enough".

The local elections of June 2004 were seen as a crucial barometer for the Government. All Government TDs were told to play a more active part than might otherwise be the case, which was probably a tall order given that in many cases, up and coming councillors would be seen as a threat by some local TDs who were already on shaky electoral ground. In Dublin South, however, that was not seen as a problem as the two Fianna Fáil TDs had built up fairly solid bases between them. But the normal "friendly" election rivalry between the Brennan and Kitt political machines was bound to come into play, as each TD vied to have their preferred candidate elected. Séamus decided to be very up-front with his support and allocated campaign teams to each of his preferred candidates – but all that effort was to have very mixed results. Of his six preferred candidates, only two were elected, while Kitt, with only two preferred candidates, saw both of them successful.

But that's politics – you take the rough with the smooth; you win some and you lose some.

In the three-seat Stillorgan Electoral Area, Séamus had a free hand (as there was no direct Kitt candidate) and supported the two Fianna Fáil candidates, Gerry Horkan and Mary White. Horkan had been co-opted to Dun Laoghaire Rathdown County Council in autumn 2003 to the seat previously held by Senator Don Lydon, who was required to resign due to the abolition of the dual mandate, while Mary White had been an official at Fianna Fáil headquarters. To distinguish her from Senator Mary White (who also lived in Dublin South), she was known within the Brennan camp as "Little Mary White". Horkan was elected to the second seat with 1,497 first preferences, but unfortunately White's support fell apart and she was eliminated.

Also with three seats was the Glencullen Electoral Area where Séamus's preference was the sitting councillor, Tommy Murphy, who had been co-opted to Dun Laoghaire Rathdown County Council in June 2002 following the death of his much respected father and long time councillor, Jimmy Murphy. The second Fianna Fáil candidate was a prominent local activist called Maria Corrigan (who would become a Taoiseach's nominee to the Seanad in 2007) and who was not particularly aligned with either Brennan or Kitt. In a remarkable result, after the Labour Party topped the poll with Lettie McCarthy on 1,941 first preferences, Corrigan took the second seat with 1,812 first preferences. Murphy, despite achieving the third highest number of first preferences (1,627), was overtaken on transfers from Labour by the outgoing Fine Gael councillor, Tom Joyce, who had received just 1,333 first preferences. This was a bitter blow to Séamus as the early prediction had been that Fianna Fáil could take two of the three seats.

Séamus's Churchtown home and constituency office were both situated smack in the middle of the Dundrum Electoral Area where there were six seats and two of the three sitting Fianna Fáil councillors were associated with him – Tony Kelly and Trevor Matthews. The third man, Tony Fox, had the personal support of Tom Kitt. But as with Glencullen, there was a surprise in store. Fox and Matthews were easily elected with first preference votes of 2,121 and 1,515 respectively, while Kelly (with 1,508) should have taken a seat but lost out to an increase in support for Fine Gael which saw their outgoing councillor, Pat Hand, just pip Kelly for the last seat. Although Séamus was delighted with the success of Matthews (who coincidentally had been co-opted some years before to the seat once held by Tom Kitt), the loss of Kelly's seat was a huge bombshell.

In the Terenure Rathfarnham Electoral Area (which cut across both Dublin South and Dublin South-Central Dáil constituencies), Tom Kitt had his most important candidate. John Lahart was an outgoing councillor and Special Adviser to Kitt, a post he had occupied previously but left only to return a couple of years later. Séamus's candidate, Vincent Kenny, was a recent recruit to Fianna Fáil and was co-opted to South Dublin County Council in the autumn of 2003 when Senator Ann Ormonde had to retire with the abolition of the dual mandate. He was also a former Progressive Democrat activist, well known in the area for his community work, most notably as the Chairman of Knocklyon Community Council and Chairman of the ad-hoc group campaigning for a second level school in Knocklyon which Séamus had previously delivered as Minister for Education, only to have it rescinded by his successor, Niamh Breathnach of Labour, and to have it brought back again through his successful lobbying of her Fianna Fáil successor, Micheál Martin. Lahart easily topped the poll with 3,828 first preferences, while expected support for Kenny did not materialise, as he received just 1,585 first preferences. This was a massive boost to Tom Kitt, and another disappointment for Dublin South's senior minister.

So the total was two for Brennan and two for Kitt, but if proof was needed, this showed that the support of a senior politician can be quite a mixed blessing for local election candidates.

Nationally, the Government parties did not do particularly well in the local and European elections, and scapegoats were being sought. There were regular commentaries in the media about who might be moved, who might be dropped, and who might be kept in what was an expected mid-term cabinet reshuffle in the autumn. With Charlie McCreevy vacating Finance to take up the post of European Commissioner, it provided at least one vacancy for the reshuffle and commentators and political groupies alike had a free run for a couple of months to indulge their fantasies.

Some of the speculation revolved around Séamus, who by this time had held eight different portfolios in Government over 17 years. In an interview with Harry McGee of the *Irish Examiner* published on 11 August 2004, Séamus decided that he would tackle the story head-on and air his views:

> A lot of my colleagues have had seven years in their Ministries. Transport is a new Department set up only two years ago. When I took it over, I embarked on a big agenda. In two years, I have achieved a lot. But there's a substantial amount of work in progress and I would like the opportunity to finish that.

Given his economic credentials and significant cabinet expertise, it was not surprising that Séamus also disclosed in that interview that he would consider moving from his beloved Transport if he was offered the post of Minister for Finance, although Harry McGee believed that it was "now almost a certainty that Brian Cowen will be offered that position". In the event, that journalistic intuition was proven right.

But it was other serious and significant comments that had caused Séamus to feel he had to go on the record.

Harry McGee wrote that Séamus was responding "to persistent speculation that he may have to make way for Tanaiste Mary Harney in the autumn by categorically stating that it was his wish to stay in Transport". Mary Harney was Minister for Enterprise, Trade and Employment at this stage and some commentators had speculated that she favoured a change, though there had been no direct suggestion from her that she had set her mind on Transport. Obviously, such speculation was a cause of concern to Séamus and those close to him. As a result, he instructed this author to check out the situation with one of Harney's advisers, Oliver O'Connor, which was done immediately and was told very clearly that there was absolutely no truth in the story as far as Harney was concerned:

> Why would she want to take over the job of a Minister who was doing reforms with which she agreed? She did want to move Departments but not to Transport.

On the day of the reshuffle, Harney took on the role of Minister for Health and Children at her own specific request to the Taoiseach, since it was known that Micheál Martin would not mind moving. For the record, it should be noted that Séamus never had a desire to occupy ministerial posts in just two of the 15 departments: Health and Agriculture. While he was relieved that neither of those was offered to him, he was bitterly disappointed when Bertie Ahern asked him to move from Transport to another department which was not Finance.

Interviewed for *The Irish Times* by Daniel McConnell some years later (August 2006), Séamus made it clear that he felt he was shafted out of Transport, despite later denials of this by Bertie Ahern:

> The dogs in the street know I would have loved to have kept going in Transport. It was the Taoiseach's decision and I was hugely disappointed with it. There is no point in trying to deceive anyone on it. I was thoroughly enjoying what I was doing and I was hugely committed to it.

It was around this time that his real zest for public life began to hit a downward spiral, and close friends believe his health also began to deteriorate partly as a result of being moved from his beloved Transport to a department that he felt he would not be "able to get to grips with".

But if he really believed that he would not "get to grips" with any department, it was the first time in his political life that he was entirely wrong.

Chapter 8

Pensions and Poverty

THE 29 SEPTEMBER 2004 RESHUFFLE saw Séamus moving from Transport to Social and Family Affairs, and while he was distinctly uneasy about it, calling it "akin to a train crashing into a wall", he fully recognised the Constitutional prerogative of the Taoiseach to appoint whoever he wished. But he genuinely felt that Bertie Ahern only moved him because he was getting too close to a final resolution of the serious issues in aviation and public transport, which had aggravated the trade union movement. They were perceived to have been using their clout with the Taoiseach to either slow down or remove the threat to their dominance of Irish aviation and transport. Of course, this was always strenuously denied by Bertie, who said that as Taoiseach, "you had to make tough choices and get on with it".

But significantly, perhaps, the attempt to downplay the transfer of Séamus was not endorsed by some people close to Bertie, and that had the effect of giving extra credibility to the early suspicion. While Séamus was well used to the up and downs of political life, he was growing tired of getting plans to a certain stage, only for them to be stalled by other political imperatives. In *Most Skilful, Most Devious, Most Cunning*, John Downing is very clear:

> The rationale behind these changes is not easy to find. But this writer's understanding is that both Harney's and Brennan's appointments are a deliberate attempt to help both to collude in softening the overall Government image.

He then goes on to quote a Government source: "Brennan's agenda will not be recanted – but it will fall into decline through a benign neglect".

Arriving at the HQ of the Department of Social and Family Affairs, Aras Mhic Dhiarmada, over Busaras in Store Street (where ironically Bus Éireann was the tenant of the Department), Séamus was pleased to find a fellow Galwegian as Secretary-General. John Hynes was originally from Gort and he was equally glad to see another Galway man as the political chief.

Once again, it was necessary for Séamus to get to know a new Private Secretary. Robert Delaney had served as Private Secretary to the two immediate predecessors, Mary Coughlan and Dermot Ahern. The two got on well from the start, helped by the fact that both had a similar sense of humour, and their special relationship was immensely helped by another staff member, Teresa McQuirk, who had worked closely with the Private Secretary and who deputised for him on occasions.

And once again, the four personal staff of this author, Mary Browne, Tom Rowley and Bobby Holland moved across the Liffey from Kildare Street to take up their posts at Aras Mhic Dhiarmada.

Despite the well known fact that he was distinctly uneasy about taking on this Department, Séamus was determined that the image of Social and Family Affairs would be enhanced during his term and that it would not be seen just as a cash dispensing Department. He wanted the Department to be the leader of social change and to look behind the welfare payments to see how life could be made better for those who depended on the State. He saw the supports from his Department as "the safety net that keeps people out of the grip of poverty and exploitation", and passionately believed that Ireland could only be proud of itself when it reached out and reached down to lift those who, for whatever reason, had been left behind or felt marginalised.

As he said in a later interview with Alison O'Connor in *The Sunday Business Post*, "I don't see any point in having a political leadership role, such as the ones that Ministers have, if you don't seek to improve and reform and change things".

The Department of Social and Family Affairs had arisen from its crusty old fashioned title of Department of Social Welfare, after a short stint as the Department of Social, Community and Family Affairs, but the "Community" role was transferred to Éamon Ó Cuiv to beef up his portfolio as Minister for Rural and Gaeltacht Affairs. For some reason, Social and Family Affairs had been seen as a sort of Governmental graveyard over the years, which was very surprising when you consider that one million people received social welfare supports. This represented the largest spend of any of the 15 Departments of State, including the Department of Health.

The first issue to be tackled was a series of 16 cutbacks (officially called adjustments) in Departmental expenditure which had been initiated by the immediate Ministerial predecessor, Mary Coughlan at the instigation of the Department of Finance. But Séamus believed there was a better way to achieve the necessary savings of some €50 million – a way which would not impact unduly on the most vulnerable people in Ireland. He began the slow process of dismantling the proposals which had to be done in a way which would not appear to be overly critical of his predecessor.

But business was business and with the usual adeptness which Séamus had shown in all other posts, he began discussions with social partners and welfare interest groups before securing cabinet approval for directing that many of the measures should be eased considerably. Some were to be the subject of specific reviews. His guiding light was that "appropriate changes would be made to any of the measures where there were indicators of hardship". This crystallised his irreverent title as "Minister for Poverty". Séamus had a new challenge and, whatever his initial personal feelings, he was not going to shirk it now.

Accepting this Ministry had been a major turning point for Séamus, the great supporter of business, competition and free enterprise. His new role as saviour of the poor defined his credentials as a caring and socially aware Minister. At one stage, Bertie Ahern told the Dáil that there were only two true socialists in the Dáil – himself and an unnamed person. Séamus always felt that he could be the other socialist, rather than anyone else who tried to portray themselves in that way, though there were several other pretenders to that throne.

He quickly began to feel at home in the Department and wanted to begin the process of confronting the social issues that consigned too many people to lives of welfare dependency. He wanted to introduce reforms to "break the shackles of welfare dependency" as he said in a speech to the Fianna Fáil Ard Fheis in 2005. He was not prepared to just oversee welfare payments and hope that "social problems would go away".

The "social problems" which he identified in that speech included taking children out of the "clutches of poverty", and "putting the children of the nation first"; pension reform, for those who "helped keep the country afloat through the decades of recession and stagnation, the people who fed, nurtured and reared the Celtic Tiger"; reforms to open up employment, training and education opportunities to "liberate thousands of lone parents from welfare constraints"; providing the necessary "structures and increased opportunities for those with disabilities"; and reviewing and updating the various schemes run by the Department and the names given to them.

These were seen as some of the core issues which many previous Ministers in the Department had either steered clear of or did not wish to pursue. He could have sat on his laurels and not rocked any boats, but that was not Séamus's way – and rock some boats he surely did.

Speaking to the Select Committee on Social and Family Affairs in Leinster House at the time of his first Budget in 2004, he told them some stark home truths:

> It is not sufficient in this economically vibrant twenty-first century Ireland to institutionalise our problems, to lock people into poverty traps, pay the bill, brag about the amount of social welfare we pay, and then convince

ourselves that this is truly progressive and enlightened social policy.

He maintained a strong personal belief, referred to many time in speeches, that future generations would not base their judgments on how many millionaires, even billionaires, were created out of Ireland's exceptional economic surges:

> They will judge us on how we honestly and sympathetically harnessed the fruits of that economic buoyancy to reach out and reach down to help and lift those who feared they were being left behind by the rising tide of economic growth. At the end of the day, what legacy could be more rewarding and more lasting than to hand on to future generations an Ireland that has eradicated social injustice? An Ireland that is free of the greatest evil of all – poverty.

In March 2005, there were two by-elections: in Kildare North due to Charlie McCreevy being appointed as European Commissioner, and in Meath due to John Bruton being appointed as EU Ambassador to Washington. One of the burning issues of those campaigns was the escalating cost of childcare and all senior Ministers were under orders to give as much time as possible to canvass with the candidates. Séamus wanted to be upfront with the electorate, which he believed should always be the case, and he said that:

> ... a lot of my colleagues, and that includes the opposition, realised a number of things they hadn't known before these by-election campaigns – finding out that people are getting up at 5.30 am, dropping the kids off at the crèche before work and not getting home again until 7.00 pm.

That was probably the nub of the issue, allied to the costs, and it showed that politicians are human, that they do not have all the answers immediately, and that they were listening to what people had to say – but the electorate in both constituencies, as usual for a Government in power, did not vote to return Fianna Fáil TDs. The Independent Catherine Murphy won in Kildare North (but was not re-elected subsequently), while Shane McEntee was the victor for Fine Gael in Meath (and retained his seat at the following general election).

Of the many issues requiring attention on his new social agenda, it was clear that the easiest would be updating several scheme names to better reflect what they did – to do what they say on the tin, so to speak. Accordingly, he was fond of saying that he had "abolished old age", because he changed the "Old Age Pension" to "State Pension", a simple move which received universal approval. But he did note in a speech to the Senior Citizens Parliament that one historical figure might not have shared his enthusiasm:

> I have to say that one David Lloyd George may not be happy with the change. He may not be spinning in his grave ... but I suspect he will be twitching a little. It was Lloyd George, as the then British Prime Minister, who was responsible in 1908 for introducing the old age pension in Ireland.
>
> In fairness to Lloyd George, he was only following the trend set by Germany's first Chancellor, Otto von Bismarck, who established the first structured pension scheme some decades before, in the 1880s. Now Otto had his own motives for bringing in pensions. His view was that, and I quote, 'anybody who has before him the prospect of a pension, be it ever so small, in old age and infirmity is much happier and more contented in his lot, much more tractable and easy to manage'.
>
> Maybe Lloyd George thought bringing in pensions would make the Irish 'easier to manage'. If he did, well he got that one badly wrong, as the events in the years that followed were to show.

Among the other changes were "Unemployment Benefit" and "Unemployment Assistance" becoming "Jobseeker's Benefit" and "Jobseeker's Assistance". He also totally removed an outdated "Unemployability Supplement" which he felt conjured up an image of someone being on the scrap heap.

Of course, these changes were more than just cosmetic, important and all as that was. He was determined to ensure that available money would be targeted more at those most in need in our society, and to that end secured significant increases in income supports for the Department's customers in each of the three Budgets he negotiated with the Minister for Finance. But he was also acutely aware that increased monetary supports were of little use on their own – they had to be augmented by encouragement, incentives and activation measures which met specific individual needs and abilities. This is what he wanted to do in getting behind the social welfare payments and to boldly go, like Star Trek, where no Minister had gone before.

The issue of pensions was one such area which he was greatly concerned about. His determination to push the pension debate was based on three irrefutable statistics:

1. From a total workforce of over two million, some 930,000 people had no provision for supplementary pensions but appeared to be relying on the State Pension.

2. By 2030, there would be almost one million persons over age 65 compared to the then current number of 464,000.

3. Four workers contribute to the support of every pensioner, which would fall to 2.7 by 2026 and to less than 1.5 by 2056.

In an address to Seanad Éireann on 18 November 2004, Séamus outlined the gravity of the situation:

> One of the miracles of the modern age has been the rapid improvement in life expectancy. Thankfully, we are all living longer, healthier and more active lives.

The number of older people in our society will increase in the years ahead and this is something which should be welcomed and celebrated and not in any way considered a burden.

The challenge we face is to provide a pensions system that will provide adequate resources for people to enjoy the type of retirement they would wish for, and which they have earned through a life-time of work. It is also important to ensure that the system is affordable in the future so that we do not place unsustainable costs on future generations and put the benefits we want for all older people, and for ourselves, in due course, at risk.

In order to further stimulate the debate on pension security for the elderly, Séamus officially wrote to the Pensions Board in February 2005 asking that they prepare a report on a supplementary pension system and to "respond without delay with urgent proposals to address the issue". They were asked to give "an analysis of international experience, lessons from abroad, on what works and what doesn't work", with the request that they report back within six months. Interviewed by Niall Brady in *The Sunday Tribune*, Séamus disclosed that he asked the Pensions Board to rip up the rule books and start again:

I've told them to be radical, to think the unthinkable, not to dodge the issue. We might never get this chance again. We cannot leave 900,000 people stranded, many of them vulnerable and facing uncertain retirements. The State requires that you have motor insurance and I believe that something similar is required for pensions.

In response, the Board formally welcomed the opportunity for involvement in this important review and confirmed that they would proceed with the work as quickly as possible with a view to making a progress report to the Minister in June and submitting the full report by September or early October 2005.

However, the Report, while it arrived almost in line with the set deadline, did not come up with a single recommendation, much to the chagrin of Séamus. He had expected that the Board, as the legal regulator of pension policy, would be more proactive in their findings and give him firm recommendations to bring to Government. After all, one of the statutory functions of the Pensions Board, as defined in their legislation, is "to advise the Minister on all matters relating to these functions and on any matters relating to pensions generally". After this, he was quite critical of the Pensions Board at meetings with officials, saying that the Board had not stepped up to the mark on this occasion, but he probably wisely resisted the temptation to say this publicly, although he went as far as he could by noting curtly in a press release that "the report is a technical examination of the practical issues".

Under the Pensions Act of 1990, the Board was composed of 17 people who were representative of trade unions, employers, Government, pension scheme trustees, the pensions industry, consumer interests, pensioner interests and the various professional groups involved with pension schemes. In many ways, the legislation facilitated a hotchpotch of a Board which made it difficult for new ideas and thoughts to come to fruition. The failure to get an agreed recommendation smacked of the old tribal differences between the various factions, particularly the tensions which bedevilled any interaction between the old protagonists of trade unions and employer representatives.

The scene was being set for another showdown between Séamus and vested interests. As Niall Brady observed in *The Sunday Tribune*:

> The pint-sized Minister's big plans for pensions reform are sure to land him back in the hot seat, igniting battles that could become every bit as ugly as his previous tussles with Aer Rianta and other parts of the State controlled transport infrastructure.

The issue this time was whether the country should have a mandatory or voluntary supplementary pension system. In order to develop the important agenda for pension reform, Séamus continually pushed the national debate which brought pension policy to the forefront, and he scored a notable success when it was included in the social partnership document, "Towards 2016".

Addressing the Annual General Meeting of the Irish Senior Citizens Parliament in April 2006, he chose his words carefully:

> Those that want to retire at 65 or 66 must do so safe in the security of a solid and consistent income from the State. Therefore, as has been the case in recent years, pensions must remain ahead of inflation and price increases. But I am also strongly of the view that empowering older people in the workplace, enabling them to choose to work longer, must also be a pivotal part of any response to the ageing challenge.

Every year there is a Social Welfare Bill in the Oireachtas which is the legal mechanism for paying social welfare increases, and is brought in within days of the Finance Minister delivering the annual Budget speech. For years, it had been known simply as the "Social Welfare (Miscellaneous Provisions) Bill", but in order to emphasise the importance of pensions, Séamus changed it to the "Social Welfare and Pensions Bill" which he believed kept the pension issue firmly in the minds of Oireachtas members and the wider public.

From Séamus's perspective, the debate was to be brought together in a Green Paper on Pensions which he hoped to publish by March 2007. But with a general election due in June 2007, the Government decided to hold publication so as not to distract from the coming election campaign. Séamus told me that delaying publication was a mistake and represented another missed opportunity to tackle a clearly identified future problem before it became a current problem.

Allied to the pension debate was the issue of carers and on identifying that 79 per cent of carers were women and 21 per cent were men, he became determined that they should receive recognition. He acknowledged that family carers were a unique group because of their work and contribution to society and for the undoubted saving they represented for the health service. In Budget 2006, he backed this line of thought by introducing a larger increase in payments to carers than other recipients of social welfare support. The following year, he went even further and brought in a Half Rate Carers Allowance for those who were on other welfare payments as "recognition of the valuable work being done".

This was a major change as it was not previously possible for people to receive two welfare payments at the same time. The initiative brought the caring issue into the forefront of political thinking, which was his major objective, and effectively put it up to the Departments of Finance and Health that it was a socially better and less expensive way of dealing with the real issue of aging and disability in the population.

In a statement issued just after the Budget, he spoke bluntly:

> Introducing the new dual payment system means we will be starting to recognise the Carers Allowance less as a welfare income payment and more as a direct support for caring duties and responsibilities.

In other speeches he continued the pursuit of that objective by committing himself to doing his part to bring forward proposals:

> ... that recognise the valued and valuable contribution of carers in a tangible way. There are many other issues being considered as regards greater opportunity, and greater mobility and travel opportunities, for older people. I have started discussions on how access to technology for older people can be greatly increased. The Internet, mobiles phones and many other devices can transform into valuable communications lifelines for older people.

The issue of an all-island free travel scheme is also moving closer to delivery from meetings North and South at Ministerial and official level.

The day he was able to announce the extension of free travel to all parts of the island of Ireland was the culmination of an exercise which extended the very successful Free Travel Scheme which had been introduced decades earlier by Charlie Haughey as Minister for Health and Social Welfare. With the peace process bedding down in the North, all Ministers had been asked to develop initiatives with a cross-border dimension and this had been set as the contribution from Séamus:

> This scheme heralds the beginning of a new era in All-Ireland travel opportunities for tens of thousands of older people on the island. It is an initiative that will remove all existing restrictions and help to build new understandings and friendships throughout the island. In many ways it is about more than just new unrestricted travel arrangements, it is a facility that will allow the older people of the island to gain a deeper understanding of each other's part of the country. It is also a recognition, and a gesture of gratitude, to all of our older people who have contributed so much over so many years to the building and shaping of the modern, progressive island we have today.

Another core issue in his social vision for the future was the pressing need for reform around the area of lone parents. In a speech to Network Galway in January 2005, he set the tone for what he hoped would be the start of a major national debate on support for lone parents, given that straight financial costs at the time absorbed about €800 million of the social welfare budget. He noted that 84 per cent of lone parents were women, and that one in every three children born in the State were to parents who were not married – in social welfare terms, they were lone parents. He posed a thought for his audience:

What has been society's response to this dramatic shift and new trend? We pay an allowance to lone parents only on condition that their partner, most often the father of the child, does not live in the same house or flat. If a lone parent seeks to work, the response is more often than not to reduce or terminate the allowance. Another disturbing aspect is that 50 per cent of lone parents have no educational qualifications past primary school. Our system effectively institutionalises lone parents and curbs attempts at a normal family life, discourages work and restricts the chances to advance educationally.

Significantly, he acknowledged that the substantial supports provided to lone parents were passive in nature, with "no active or systematic supports in assisting the take-up of education, training or employment opportunities". He then went on to state quite bluntly that a lone parent:

... can continue to receive their payment until their child is 18, or 22 if in full time education, with no direct intervention by the State. This long term welfare dependency is not in the best interests of the lone parent, their children, or society in general.

In an address at a Dublin hotel for International Women's Day, Séamus went further in his efforts to keep the issue of lone parents to the forefront:

I want to debunk some of the myths about lone parents. This is essentially pub talk, coming from the high stool experts. I want to state some facts and put the record straight.

Of lone parents, 84 per cent are women, 16 per cent are men. In reality, less than 3 per cent, 2.8 per cent to be exact, of lone parents are teenagers. The notion that there is an army of teenagers is not accurate. In fact, 75 per cent of all lone parents are over 25 and the average

age is approximately 27 or 28, one-third of lone parents are in their 30s.

The other myth is that lone parents have a multiplicity of children because there is great money to be had from the system. This is also inaccurate, as 60 per cent have one child and 25 per cent have two. In other words, 85 per cent of lone parents have two children or fewer.

Lone parents tend to be older than pub talk suggests and tend to have one child. This gives the lie to the myth that somehow there is a racket going on as the figures show clearly this is not the case.

Lone parents have genuine pressures and our job is to meet those pressures.

Now the cat was well and truly among the pigeons. But all the straight talking seemed to have brought results when he published a document called "Proposals for Supporting Lone Parents and Low Income Families", which attempted to analyse the practical difficulties experienced by many of the 80,000 such families with 130,000 children. Areas he had addressed in the Galway speech – like access to employment, education and training, income supports, childcare and cohabitation rules – were all now in the mix for discussion. While receiving a generally supportive response from representative organisations, there was concern about how realistic the plans were for the non-income support issues.

He said at the launch of the document:

Lone parents have to carry the double burden of providing for the care of their children and being the sole family breadwinner. As a result, fewer than half of lone parents are in employment and as we all know, a high percentage of lone parent families are categorised as 'at risk of poverty'.

I firmly believe that one of the most effective routes out of poverty for lone parents is through paid employment.

Indeed, one of the objectives of the one parent family payment is to encourage lone parents to consider employment as an alternative to welfare dependency.

The reform proposals are not about bringing about savings – they are about introducing a more enlightened social policy that directly targets and benefits the lives of tens of thousands of people, especially children.

Of course, access to employment brings its own difficulties. Reconciling work and family life is a major problem for one parent families.

It is therefore crucial that priority is given to further developing the supports available to lone parents who opt to work outside the home in enabling them to meet both the demands of work and care for family.

One of the leading national organisations for one-parent families in Ireland, One Family (formerly Cherish), stated that they had a "very positive relationship" with Séamus as he was "involved in progressing positive initiatives aimed at improving the lives of the most vulnerable people in our society through changes in the social welfare system".

But another leading representative body for lone parents, OPEN, identified some practical difficulties, particularly in relation to "stimulating access to employment which represents a major challenge to a number of Government Departments".

Meanwhile, Terry Prone in the *Sunday Tribune* wrote of Séamus being "one of the few talking about the quantum shift in Irish society". But she had a little sting in the tail:

Séamus Brennan is a lot more interesting now than he was when he was younger. Which is unexpected. Most politicians, as they age, just get more like themselves. Road to Damascus conversions are rare in politics.

Having delved into the issue, and then bringing it so far, he was disappointed that it could not have been tackled head-on and resolved during his time at Social and Family Affairs. With the previous stigma of being a lone parent a thing of the past, he felt some disillusionment that the cycle of poverty which was identified in the report had brought up a whole host of related issues which the State apparatus seemed incapable of resolving any time soon. That debate is still going on.

Another area of reform which eluded him, much to his displeasure, was the amount spent by the State on temporary housing, which was quantified at more than €40 million per year, and paid mainly to private landlords throughout the country. He felt this did not effectively serve the basic needs of the homeless, who were fellow citizens and entitled to have a permanent roof over their heads. As this amount was likely to increase rather than decrease, he put out feelers for changing the scheme to either allow the State to directly purchase properties which would then be made available as temporary housing, or to develop an enhanced mortgage subsidy scheme which would allow more people, over time, to acquire their own homes. While some progress was made, it did not go as far as he wished, concentrating only on automatically transferring those on local authority housing lists after five years rather than taking any radical step to achieve better value for the taxpayers' huge subsidy.

Of the three Budgets which Séamus presided over during his term at Social and Family Affairs, the 2006 Budget was the most memorable. It marked a new phase in Séamus's career as a Minister when he put it up to the Minister for Finance, Brian Cowen, that whatever else was done, substantial money had to be provided for pensioners and the less well off. In his book *Cowen: The Path to Power*", Jason O'Toole quoted Cowen at that time: "I want to help those on lower incomes and to support families at all levels". This statement was directly attributable to the negotiating skills which Séamus had brought to bear on Minister Cowen and saw the completion of the commitment in the Programme for Government that pensions should reach €200 per week. In the event, Contributory Pensions were tagged at €207 per week, a move which made Séamus the darling of those over age 65 – especially his mother, Tess Brennan, who despite advancing age used to text him regularly with snippets of advice from the elderly people in Galway.

And it was the needs of the elderly that occupied a lot of his thinking. In speech after speech, he relentlessly spoke up for pensioners, whom he paternally called "our people in their later years". He was keenly aware of their need to retire with dignity (if they wanted to retire that is) and with security. In an address to a conference in Ballinlough, Co. Roscommon (close to his father's ancestral roots on Clawinch Island, Lough Rea), he was especially poignant:

> Some of our most vulnerable older people are the men and women on Non-Contributory State Pensions who receive less every week than those on Contributory Pensions, and are also subject to employment restrictions. I note that over 40 per cent of all those now on these pensions live in the Border/Midlands/Western region.
>
> In the last Budget, I took a first step towards closing the pension's gap and also increased the earnings ceiling from €7 to €100 a week for Non-Contributory Pensions. I am determined to continue to work towards improving the incomes, and opportunities, for these pensioners.

If speeches and media output were the marker of activity, then Séamus would have been very high on the scale. During his tenure in Social and Family Affairs, he issued 171 official press releases and made 51 formal scripted speeches, apart altogether from off the cuff comments at functions and public meetings where a formal script was not required, along with media door-stepping. But such a work rate was not unusual for him. In December 2002, Niamh Connolly in a lengthy piece for The Sunday Business Online (ThePost.ie) said that he had been "compared to the Duracell bunny for a relentless stream of public announcements".

From being annoyed at having to move from his beloved Department of Transport, Séamus quickly became passionate about the marginalised, those in poverty and those in danger of being left behind. It was as if he had found a true vocation in attempting to deal with the real problems and issues affecting those who have to depend on social welfare. A favourite quotation which Séamus used in many speeches was a play on a quotation attributed to that legendary American financier, Warren Buffet, who said:

> A rising tide lifts all boats. It's only when the tide goes out that you learn who's been swimming naked.

Séamus refined that to say in regard to those citizens of Ireland who depend on social welfare, "A rising tide does not lift all boats" – and he believed it was his solemn duty as Social and Family Affairs Minister to help bring about a situation where the original quotation could be spoken in Ireland with complete honesty. In what seemed at first glance to be a significant compliment for Séamus, Taoiseach Bertie Ahern told him privately: "If I had known you were so good in Social and Family Affairs, I would have put you there years ago."

But perhaps that was really a back-handed compliment because after the coming election, Séamus would once again change portfolios under Bertie Ahern's third successive Government.

Chapter 9

Last Post

BERTIE AHERN'S SECOND FULL TERM as Taoiseach was coming up to the five years' mark and a general election was called for 24 May 2007. In Dublin South, Séamus had a campaign team of strategists who had been working for months. At one of the regular meetings, Séamus, as always, had his thoughts ready and had a number of bullet points on a piece of paper in front of him – such as Finance, Literature, Canvass and at the end of his list were the letters "www". This related to his desire to use the internet more strategically during the coming campaign. A long-time friend and key team member, Bob Manson Jr., recalls noticing the letters on the sheet of paper and wondering what Séamus had in mind. It quickly became clear when Séamus, who always chaired his team meetings, "volunteered" Bob to examine how the internet could be utilised. But it was not just a random team member that Séamus had selected. Bob had significant personal experience of working on Democratic Party campaigns in the United States directly with Senator Ted Kennedy (and would later do so with President Barack Obama).

When the general election votes were counted, Séamus once again topped the poll with 13,373 first preference votes, while Tom Kitt (8,487), Olivia Mitchell (8,037) and Eamon Ryan (6,768) were also re-elected. The local surprise this time was that the Progressive Democrat's Liz O'Donnell lost her seat with 4,045 first preference votes, representing less than half of her vote from the 2002 election. Her defeat allowed Alan Shatter (Fine Gael) to slip back into the seat he lost five years before with 5,752 first prefer-

ence votes compared to his losing tally in 2002 of 5,363 first preference votes.

The full aftermath of the election was inconclusive in that no
single party achieved a majority on its own. Bob Manson Jr. recalled a prophetic conversation with Séamus a year before the
election which showed how his keen mind was thinking and how
he had an almost prophetic-like vision for the future:

> He took out a piece of paper, like the proverbial back of
> an envelope, and worked out his forecast that the Green
> Party would be in Government with Fianna Fáil – he was
> correct numbers-wise down to the last three seats in a
> Fianna Fáil/Progressive Democrats/Green Party total. It
> was fascinating and very revealing to subsequently see
> his prediction coming about.

Bertie Ahern was keen to break the mould by being the first
outgoing Taoiseach since Eamon de Valera to be returned as Taoiseach for an unprecedented third term so he set up his teams to
negotiate with the Progressive Democrats, the Green Party and
sympathetic Independents.

This was a major departure for Fianna Fáil which previously
had mixed experiences with only one coalition partner at a time –
the Progressive Democrats and the Labour Party – equivalent to
political monogamy. Now there was to be a possibility of political
polygamy with the introduction of the Green Party into the mix.
This new and radical variation for Fianna Fáil required negotiators with level heads who could be depended on to do the right
thing if there was to be a successful political marriage. Once again,
it was time to call on the "safe pair of hands" – Séamus Brennan
joined Brian Cowen and Noel Dempsey for the negotiations with
John Gormley, Eamon Ryan and Dan Boyle. Author and political
journalist John Cooney would later write that "Séamus was the
brains behind Bertie's pact with the Greens".

Of course, it was a new situation for the Green Party as well,
and it has passed into political legend that Séamus said to the
Green representatives at the beginning of the discussions: "You

are playing senior hurling now lads – but you are playing with lads with All-Ireland medals". That one statement probably defined the scene and brought the negotiations on to a new plane of encouragement, facilitation and straight talking. It was inherent in Séamus's nature that he would bring about solutions, wherever possible. He often said that he was "not interested in problems, only solutions". After the election, he had managed to get hold of John Gormley's mobile phone number and sent him a flurry of text messages. Eventually, they spoke on the phone and it was only then that the Green Party began to realise that the offers of negotiation and possible political marital relations with Fianna Fáil were actually serious approaches.

They then endured many long and necessarily tedious hours at Séamus's office in Government Buildings until a mutually acceptable agreement was worked out and history was made. As Séamus said on another occasion:

> The best negotiations are often when nobody gets everything they want but everyone can hold their head high and have got something from the negotiations that their members can be happy with. I don't expect everyone to be ecstatic about any negotiations, but I do think we can arrive at satisfactory conclusions.

Séamus was highly impressed with the positive attitude which the Green Party negotiators adopted and it gave him, and many others close to Government, a much greater respect for their policies. He forecast that they would have a definite influence on the whole Government and could not understand the critics, often from within the Green Party itself, who said that the Greens would not achieve anything as a result of coalition in Government. He always had the belief that it was possible to achieve much more in Government than on the Opposition benches. He had the same pragmatic and philosophical view that he showed in accepting ten ministerial roles over the years, which were sometimes senior posts and sometimes junior ones. The kernel of the matter was that Government policy would greatly encompass so-called "green issues" which might have been alien to many people before Green Party involvement in "senior hurling". And the country would be better in the long term as a result.

While he had great respect for the Progressive Democrats, particularly most of the individuals in it, he felt that the Green Party would have a more stable future in Irish political life. The Progressive Democrats were originally founded on disgruntlement and their policies in general were not really a million miles from Fianna Fáil – nor indeed from Fine Gael – with some notable exceptions. The Green Party, on the other hand, had their own distinctive brand and individual policies which were not the preserve of any other party, although many aspects of their policies were taken on board by other parties even before the arrival of Green ministers, which probably made it much easier for Fianna Fáil to agree a Programme for Government with them. After Séamus's death, the Green Party Leader and Minister for the Environment and Local Government, John Gormley, recalled that "it has been rightly said that he played an important role in the formation of this Government – in fact, he played the pivotal role in the formation of this Government".

However, the inclusion of the Green Party in coalition talks must have been unnerving for the much reduced Progressive Democrats with only two TDs returned to the Dáil. They were preparing for life on the Opposition benches but Bertie Ahern did not want to say goodbye to the person who had been his loyal Tanaiste for a decade, Mary Harney, with whom he had an extraordinarily amicable working relationship. Mary Harney's successor, Michael McDowell, was not in the same league for his short time as Tanaiste and the working relationship would certainly have been frostier had McDowell retained his seat. On a personal level, Bertie felt it would be dishonourable to exclude Mary Harney and insisted on the PDs being part of his third administration. Of course, there was an ulterior political motive in keeping the PDs on board – they would not be able to join the Opposition and they would help to provide a bulwark in the event that the Green Party pulled out of Government early. As an added security for his Government, he sought the support of a number of Independents using the template which Séamus had in place as Chief Whip for the 1997 to 2002 minority Government.

The third successive Government led by Bertie Ahern, with Brian Cowen as Tanaiste this time, was composed of Fianna Fáil, the Progressive Democrats and the Green Party and came into office on June 14. In the new regime, Séamus had not expected nor did he actually wish to be moved from Social and Family Affairs, but the Taoiseach wanted to change around his team.

But did Bertie decide that Séamus had once again rattled vested interests with his reforming zeal on pensions, lone parents and so on? Or had Séamus accomplished as much as he could to relieve the nation's poverty? That is one of the great unanswered questions of political life and joins the list of other unanswered questions during Séamus's unique record of serving in ten ministerial positions over a period of 21 years.

As it happened, the outgoing Minister for Arts, Sport and Tourism, John O'Donoghue, became Ceann Comhairle. His post was therefore available to the Taoiseach and Séamus accepted it on the basis that he had previously been Tourism Minister and liked the challenge of taking up the cudgels for Arts and Sport, while resuming his interest in the important tourism sector. In a previous incarnation of the Department, Jim McDaid as Minister had been dubbed "Minister for Fun", but this was an accolade that Séamus did not want for himself and he went to great strides to remove the idea from circulation.

The new Private Secretary was Therese O'Connor who was to be succeeded some months later by Gary McGuinn. The team of this author, Mary Browne, Tom Rowley and Bobby Holland made the move from the north side of the Liffey to Kildare Street, thus completing the circle back to the building where Séamus (along with the first two) began his ministerial career 20 years earlier.

This was a small department of about 180 people, half of which had decentralised to Killarney. The final move of the rest of the department to Killarney was scheduled for the end of 2008 – the first department to move entirely to a location outside the capital

– but Séamus was concerned that such a move would be logisti-
cally difficult for him as a minister representing a Dublin constituency. It would make better sense for a significant senior presence
to remain in Dublin, which would not only benefit any future minister, but also make the job of Government easier given the need
for ministers to be accessible to the capital city. This was decentralisation gone stark, raving mad and Séamus was prepared to
fight it. He instructed his officials to convey his views and he was
prepared to address it at cabinet level at the appropriate time.

His concerns on decentralisation had actually been aired when
the Green Party were in opposition just two years earlier. Dan
Boyle (who was then a TD and subsequently became a Taoiseach's
nominee to the Seanad) called decentralisation "a policy born out
of nothing other than seeking political advantage" and he had
gone on to twist the knife he had just stuck in:

> From the moment of Charlie McCreevy's announcement
> in his final budget speech, this has been a policy riddled
> with contradictions. It directly opposed the now equally
> discredited National Spatial Strategy. It created mayhem
> in the workforces, particularly of semi-state agencies. It
> created only a demand for civil and public servants
> already working outside of the Dublin area to move to
> other parts of the country. From a Green Party point of
> view, this Government policy has peddled a perverse and
> pointless definition of decentralisation that has under-
> mined the potential that decentralisation can and should
> play in regional development.

But it proved difficult to get other ministers and their officials
to put their heads above the parapet with him. Even the Green
Party ministers were nowhere to be seen on this issue. It seemed
that because other departments were not immediately threatened,
their ministers were prepared to sit it out and see what happened
when Arts, Sport and Tourism made the final break.

Meanwhile, as a TD, Séamus had a vote in the Seanad election
and went over the list of candidates as thoroughly, as strategically,

and as surgically as he would if he was a candidate looking for votes himself. But for some reason on this occasion, he was particularly keen that his preferences in the 2007 election would be accurately preserved and released at the appropriate time when he was no longer involved in politics. Was this a premonition? I don't know, but keeping to his request, the Seanad preferences were as follows:

Cultural & Educational Panel:
1. Ann Ormonde, Dublin; 2. Paschal Mooney, Leitrim; 3. Tony McKenna, Tipperary; 4. Paul Kelly, Kildare; 5. John Brassil, Kerry; 6. Aidan Crowley, Mayo; 7. Frank Maher, Louth; 8. Labhras O Murchu, Tipperary.

Industrial & Commercial Panel:
1. Eddie Bohan, Dublin; 2. Brendan Kenneally, Waterford; 3. Margaret Cox, Galway; 4. Tom Moffatt, Mayo; 5. March MacSharry, Sligo; 6. Gerard Killaly, Offaly; 7. Larry Butler, Dun Laoghaire; 8. Pat O'Meara, Tipperary; 9. Michael Regan, Galway; 10. Val Hanley, Galway; 11. Mary White, Dublin; 12. Kieran Phelan, Laois; 13. Gerry Bridgett, Kildare; 14. Michael Cahill, Kerry; 15. Aidan Colleary, Sligo; 16. John Egan, Tipperary; 17. Ted Fitzgerald, Kerry; 18. Brendan Hughes, Monaghan; 19. Michael McGrath, Cork; 20. Kevin O'Keeffe, Cork.

Agricultural Panel:
1. Peter Callinan, Cork; 2. Frank Chambers, Mayo; 3. Mary Hoade, Galway; 4. Jim Walsh, Wexford; 5. Pat Moylan, Offaly; 6. Donagh Mark Killilea, Galway; 7. Paddy McGowan, Donegal; 8. Tom Fleming, Kerry; 9. Albert Higgins, Sligo; 10. Francie O'Brien, Monaghan; 11. Rory Kiely, Limerick.

Administrative Panel:
1. Tony Kett, Dublin; 2. Michael Kitt, Galway; 3. Marian McGennis, Dublin; 4. Diarmuid Wilson, Cavan; 5. Camillus Glynn,

Westmeath; 6. Timmy Dooley, Clare; 7. Enda Bonner, Donegal; 8. Enda Nolan, Carlow.

Labour Panel:
1. Don Lydon, Dublin; 2. Brendan Daly, Clare; 3. Terry Leyden, Roscommon; 4. Geraldine Feeney, Sligo; 5. Eddie Wade, Limerick; 6. Liam Fitzgerald, Dublin; 7. John Hanafin, Tipperary; 8. Garry Keegan, Dublin; 9. Rody Kelly, Carlow; 10. Dan Kiely, Kerry; 11. Sean Collins, Louth.

The previous Minister for Arts, Sport and Tourism, John O'Donoghue, had a part-time Arts Adviser, Donal Shiels, whose contract (like all advisers) had ceased with the change of Government. The arts community seemed to value having a designated arts adviser with the ear of the minister, but Séamus decided that he did not need to have a specific person in that role, as the arts community themselves, combined with the experienced people in the department, were more than capable of dealing with advice on the arts. He duly met with the representatives of the arts and acquainted them with this new policy, assuring them that they had his ear if they wanted it.

When the Fine Gael front bench was announced, Séamus was intrigued to see that his constituency colleague, Olivia Mitchell, was to shadow him. It was unusual to have a minister shadowed by an opposition colleague in the same constituency and it led to Olivia making a comment to me that "I can't be too hard on him – I know he is more popular than I am". But Olivia was seen within the local Fianna Fáil machine as "the acceptable face of Fine Gael", unlike her party colleague, Alan Shatter, who was considered to be remote, unfriendly and "a bit of a b......s".

Book launches are regular occurrences for any political personage and Séamus was no exception to this. As Arts Minister, he took a special delight in being asked to officiate at these events. One such launch was in September 2007 for Martina Devlin's *Ship of Dreams*. The book was described by Séamus as "perhaps her most unusual one" as it drew its inspiration from when she discovered quite by chance that her great grand-uncle, Tom O'Brien from Limerick, was a passenger on the Titanic, eloping with a young woman, Hannah, who was pregnant, although his family appeared to be unaware of this. Tom drowned when the Titanic hit the iceberg but Hannah survived to safely reach New York. As always on these occasions, Séamus's quick wit found a humorous angle:

> I see that the invitation to the launch invited you all to board the "Ship of Dreams", captained by the Minister for Arts, Sport and Tourism. Now, the truth is that us politicians can be a superstitious lot at times, so I'm assuming that making a Minister the Captain of the launch of a book based around the sinking of the Titanic does not have any political undercurrents that I'm unaware of. As most of you know, I have been navigating the choppy, sometimes stormy, political waters for a good many years and so far, I have managed to steer clear of the icebergs.

But following that quip about steering clear of icebergs, he was about to see another iceberg coming his way in the form of the Arts Council, and its Chairwoman, Olive Braiden.

Séamus was concerned about the growing independent streak which was manifesting itself at the Arts Council. Olive Braiden had been appointed by the previous minister, and had previously been added as a Fianna Fáil European election candidate in 1994 at the behest of Séamus when he was part-time unpaid Director of Organisation for Fianna Fáil. As Arts Minister now, he felt very strongly that the department should be seen as the major supporter of the arts rather than the Arts Council, which after all received its funding directly from the department.

The Arts Council, however, seemed to have a different view of this and in their pre-Budget submission for 2007, they sought a grant of €100 million which would be exclusively under their control, and which was a huge leap from their 2006 Budget allocation. This irked both Séamus and officials in the department who held the view that the full picture on the Government's support for arts was being distorted as the message being put forth was that the Arts Council was the chief mechanism for arts support, and this took no account of the direct assistance given by the department through other schemes and tax benefits. For the record, the investment in the arts area broke down in the 2008 Budget as follows:

- Overall investment of almost €245 million – an increase of 6.6 per cent in the combined allocation for the arts, culture and film areas, including the National Gallery and the National Cultural Institutions

- Arts Council funding package of €85.1 million – a doubling of the touring fund, included in this, to increase access to arts and culture which was another feature of the Council's increased funding

- Current funding for the arts, culture and film area was up 5.25 per cent on 2007, 16.3 per cent on 2006, 33 per cent on 2005 and 67 per cent on 2004.

- In the five years from 2003 to 2008, current funding for the arts grew by 112 per cent (or more than doubled)

- Investment of €40 million in arts and culture infrastructural enhancement schemes

- Funding increases for cultural institutions ranging from 6 per cent to 11 per cent, including National Library and Museum, Irish Museum of Modern Art, National Concert Hall, the Crawford Gallery and the Chester Beatty Library

- Culture Ireland funding up 6 per cent to €4.75 million, enabling greater marketing of Irish arts and artists abroad

- €23.2 million allocation for the Film Board – an increase of 18 per cent – targeted at attracting international projects to Ireland

- Section 481 tax relief incentive for film and television productions in Ireland extended to 2012.

This show of strength by Séamus and his department evidently worked, although Olive Braiden, clearly stung by the new policy, was muted in her subsequent statement which said she was "pleased with the outcome". Meanwhile, Tania Banotti (a daughter of former Member of the European Parliament, Mary Banotti and a niece of former Justice Minister Nora Owen) came out in stronger support:

> This Budget was very tricky, so well done to the Minister for getting us there with a short lead-in time. The 'begging bowl' for the arts at the Government table is gone.

In the *Irish Independent's* Review of 2007, published on 22 December 2007, Séamus was brought back to his previous ministry when he was dubbed as "Minister of the Year". The accompanying write-up said that he was "the clear winner", as during his time as Minister for Social and Family Affairs, "he pretty much kept all the promises".

One area of the arts which eluded Séamus was his wish to set up an Irish Film Commission with a defined timescale to chart the way forward for the Irish film industry. Since being reconstituted in 1993, the Irish Film Board was Ireland's national film agency, charged with supporting and promoting the Irish film industry and the use of Ireland as a location for international production. Following a meeting with the Film Board, he formed the view that it had become a rather stuffy State board which was stuck in a rut, had few fresh ideas and, despite some notable successes, was unlikely to reinvigorate what was seen as a declining film industry in Ireland.

But Séamus believed they could do more and he wanted to develop a more energetic blueprint for the future. To that end, he authorised contacts with a number of big names in film who had Irish connections, including actor Gabriel Byrne and producer

Neil Jordan. He subsequently met with them to go over his plans but events overtook him before he could complete this vision.

Prior to becoming a senior minister, Séamus regularly played golf and tennis whenever he had a spare moment, though the spare moments were becoming fewer and fewer as he moved through his unique range of portfolios over the years. But he did have a passionate interest in all sports, a passion which he once said that "Ireland was renowned for". But his own passion for sport was passed to him by his mother, Tess Brennan, who was described by Kernan Andrews in the *Galway Advertiser* as "something of a soccer pioneer". Séamus often said that "the Brennan family roots go deep when it comes to sport". He was referring to his mother, who for many years was the driving force behind Salthill Devon Football Club. "As far as I know, she was the first woman to be elected President of a soccer club", he proudly proclaimed.

He once charmed an audience of international sports journalists by recalling that his first (and last) time as a soccer player himself was in the Collinwood Cup during the 1969/70 season. It seems that he was told that he "was more interested in devising the tactics for the game than in actually playing". That explains why he hung up his boots to try his luck on the political field. But his "tactics" expertise would prove to be extremely useful over the following years.

His belief was that one of the greatest attractions of sport was in helping us to escape from the business of everyday living:

> It can lift us away from the workplace, away from the daily pressures, and away briefly every now and then, from the world of politics. But I think it would be hard to convince those glued to Ireland's Triple Crown victory in rugby over England that politics, and not the clinging influence of history, was forgotten on that day.

But it was not just the main sports that Séamus wanted to foster. He was also keen to develop his knowledge of other sporting areas. To that end, he went to see a croquet match and talked to

Signing book of condolences following a fatal bus accident, 2004

Computer training for people with a disability, Colaiste Ide, Finglas, 2006

On Yer Bike – Dublin to Galway charity cycle by students from UCD, 2004

Pre-Budget talk with CORI's Fr Sean Healy, 2004

Press conference announcing 2005 Budget as Minister for Social and Family Affairs

Announcing removal of travel restrictions for pensioners, 2005

*Fianna Fáil Ard Fheis, 2006 – Mary Coughlan on right
and the author, Frank Lahiffe, in back*

*One of many press conferences – as Minister for Transport with Peter Malone,
Chairman, National Roads Authority, 2003*

At 2006 Pensions Forum with Anne Maher and Tiernan O'Mahoney

2007 press conference at Government Buildings – Mary Harney on left

Receiving Seal, as Minister for Arts, Sport and Tourism,
with President Mary McAleese and Taoiseach Bertie Ahern, 2007

Dermot Ahern and Séamus, 2007

Séamus with Micheál Martin, 2007

Making a point in 2007 election campaign

Cabinet Ministers receiving Seals of Office, 2007

Last election poster, 2007

*Relaxing in early January 2008 with (from left) sister Carmel,
daughter Sine, daughter Aoife, and her son Calum*

his long time friend, Eoin O'Brien, about cricket. Eoin was a fount
of knowledge on all matters pertaining to cricket and soon after
his appointment as Sports Minister, Séamus told Eoin that he
wanted him to be his "cricket guru" to keep him up to date on all
that was happening in the various test matches and to teach him
the terminology of cricket supporters.

On one occasion, he blended his art and sport responsibilities
by quoting Ernest Hemingway's assertion that:

> ... there are only three real sports: bull-fighting, car
> racing and mountain climbing. All the others are mere
> games. If you stick strictly to Hemingway's, dare I say
> 'bullish' pronouncement on the three real sports, then
> Ireland has been fairly good at car-racing over the years;
> our mountain climbers have scaled a few lofty peaks; but
> for some reason, the bull-fighting has never really taken
> off. Maybe it's something to do with our mild tem-
> perament and lack of interest in contact sports!

The *Galway Advertiser* recalls that he drew parallels between
politics and football:

> One day, you're on the left wing; and then before you
> know, you wake up one day to find yourself being
> described as an emerging right-winger; not to mention,
> of course, the never ending battle to avoid having
> political own goals scored against you.

He was particularly keen on the evolving National Sports
Campus at Abbotstown, which had a chequered history through it
being linked in the public mind with the abandoned "Bertie Bowl"
(an 80,000-seat national stadium which was abandoned in 2004
after opposition by the coalition partner, the Progressive Democrats). He had told Dan Flinter, Chairman of the National Sports
Campus Development Authority, that he wanted to move the project away from any suggestion that its image was tarnished, as the
development was now a million miles from the previous incarna-

tion. It was expected to provide modern facilities, including pitches and support services, for the three major field sports of rugby, soccer and Gaelic games, with shared core facilities including accommodation, fitness area, and medical and gym amenities. Facilities were also to be provided to cater for over 30 indoor sports including badminton, basketball, bowling, boxing, judo and table tennis. Community playing pitches and support conveniences were also planned for the new project.

For the formal announcement in Abbotstown, he drew together an array of sporting personalities including GAA President Nickey Brennan, GAA Director-General Pauric Duffy, Kilkenny hurler Henry Sheflin, Dublin footballer Bryan Cullen, Ireland's rugby captain Brian O'Driscoll and former international goalkeeper Packie Bonner.

It was a proud moment to be Irish, to be Sports Minister and a Dublin South TD when Padraig Harrington won the 2007 British Open and Séamus noted in a statement that:

> ... all of Ireland is extremely proud of Padraig Harrington's achievement in winning one of the world's most prestigious sporting events and in bridging the 60 years gap since Fred Daly's famous victory in the Championship.

He also revealed at the time that he had spoken to Padraig within hours of the win and:

> ... passed on to him the heartiest congratulations of the Taoiseach, the entire Government and the people of Ireland. Hailing as he does from Stackstown Golf Club in my own South Dublin constituency, I am doubly pleased and proud of his magnificent achievement.

But there was a disappointment in store. It was traditional for sporting excellence to be recognised by the Government and Séamus had arranged for the Taoiseach to host a small welcome home ceremony in Government Buildings at a time that suited Padraig, and local information confirmed that Padraig would be in Ireland some weeks later. As the proposed time came nearer, with no word from Padraig and no response to messages, Séamus dispatched this author and Media Adviser Tom Rowley to go to Padraig's home in south Dublin. They duly arrived at his home and met with members of the household who advised that Padraig was out but would be back later. They carried a personal handwritten letter from Séamus and left it and Séamus's mobile number, repeating that other messages had been sent, and asked that a call be made directly to Séamus as soon as possible.

Now one might imagine that an offer of meeting with the Head of Government, whatever your political views, to celebrate a great achievement would be snapped up, but that was not what happened. It seems that Padraig's British management would not allow him to avail of the offer for some reason – which was never made clear – but what *was* clear was that Séamus and the Taoiseach were both highly annoyed at what was seen as a snub to the State. The offer was not going to be made again.

But there were other athletes Séamus had special time for – those involved in the Special Olympics. He was particularly supportive of the Irish team in Shanghai and was bitterly disappointed when illness prevented him from travelling to see the athletes in action in November 2007. But true to form, he was not going to let the athletes feel that they did not matter. He arranged for Minister of State Sean Power to deputise for him at the events in Shanghai, accompanied by this author, Private Secretary Therese O'Connor, and Assistant Secretary-General at the Department of Arts, Sport and Tourism, Donagh Morgan. It was with great pride that Séamus was able to personally meet the athletes on their triumphant homecoming at Dublin Airport.

Séamus's sports philosophy was for supports to filter all down the line to local bodies and individuals. Visiting Abbotstown on 5 December 2007 to officially open the new headquarters of the Football Association of Ireland, Séamus outlined his vision for sport:

> Sport brings people together. It opens up opportunities, raises aspirations, builds strong and enduring friendships and benefits society in a thousand different ways. Put simply, sport has a key role in shaping lives, especially those of our young people, for the better. As Minister for Sport, I want to work with the FAI, and the other sports bodies, to greatly increase involvement and participation in sport for all of our people, regardless of social background and regardless of nationality.

Moving on from his gesture for peace as Minister for Social and Family Affairs, when he brought in the extension of free travel to all parts of the island of Ireland, he had a further opportunity to develop cross-border relations when he travelled to Belfast for the first Irish stage of the World Rally and met with First Minister Ian Paisley as they jointly started off the race in the presence of Princess Anne. His impression of Paisley was of a man who was in his element, at the peak of his political career, though also in its twilight, and who did not seem to be the ogre that many had previously thought. As the cars roared around the Stormont Buildings complex, Ian Paisley turned to Séamus and said quietly, "I don't care much for the noise".

Rally Ireland 2007 was the first ever round of the World Rally Championship to be held in Ireland and it was estimated that it was seen by some 150,000 spectators and a global TV audience of up to 50 million people in some 180 countries. Séamus viewed it as both a sporting and tourism occasion.

It was as Tourism Minister that Séamus recalled his previous period with that responsibility. But this time around, it was a different era. From a consumer perspective, aviation was moving forward after the initial downturn following the events in the United States as a result of the tragic 9/11 situation, although the airline industry might take a different view. Ryanair and Aer Lingus were going head to head for customers with low fares the order of the day, and Aer Arran was continuing in its own market segment. City Jet, which had begun operations in 1994 before being taken over by Air France in 2000, was offering flights to a number of British and European airports with short runways, which the other carriers were not able to service.

Tourism figures were strong (up 4.5 per cent on the previous record year) thanks to the combined efforts of the twin tourism bodies, Failte Ireland under Chief Executive Shawn Quinn, and the North/South body, Tourism Ireland, under its Chief Executive Paul O'Toole (who also happened to be a constituent of Séamus Brennan). One of his last acts for Tourism was attending the prestigious World Travel Fair in London in November 2007 at which Tourism Ireland had a major presence. This fair was described as "the largest trade event in the global tourism calendar year" and the optimum benefit for Ireland was achieved by the announcement of a recent survey by Lonely Planet that Ireland topped the poll as the "World's Friendliest Country".

In a Christmas statement, Séamus said:

> Tourism, and the hospitality industry in general, has contributed enormously to the overall economic growth and prosperity of the country and is arguably our biggest employer with up to 250,000 people working in these areas. We now have over 7 million visitors each year and an industry generating over €6 billion to the economy.

A humourous aside comes to mind that while Séamus was being photographed at an official tourism function in Dublin's Shelbourne Hotel, the photographer from Maxwells asked Séamus to go out a window onto the balcony to get a photograph with more light. As an obliging photographic subject, Séamus did as he was asked – but the resulting photograph (published in several newspapers) was of Séamus climbing through the window which gave the impression that he was escaping from the function. And no doubt, there were many other functions where he would have liked that opportunity.

On the home political patch, Séamus came out publicly against the continuation of what was known as "The Tent" at Galway Races. This was a massive fundraising event run by Fianna Fáil, generating a significant five to six figure sum each year, but it had become tainted by debates about the appropriateness of such fundraising. In effect, it had run its course and Séamus felt that it should be discontinued, calling it "a lightning rod for controversy". His recommendation was to be taken on board by the new Taoiseach, Brian Cowen, on 22 May 2008 when "The Tent" was formally abolished.

As an alumni of University College Galway, Séamus took great pleasure in being awarded the NUI Galway Award for Law, Public Service and Government in March 2008 at a glittering ceremony in the Galway Radisson SAS Hotel. The citation spoke of being a leader in his profession and one who excelled in his pursuits.

But it was also at this time that people began to realise that Séamus Brennan was quite ill. While illness had some effect on his work rate, he was determined to continue his public work as long as it was possible to do so.

His last public engagement outside Dublin was on 21 April 2008 when he fulfilled a long standing commitment to his Dáil colleague, Peter Kelly TD of Longford. The occasion, which seemed to have all of the village of Abbeylara present, was the official opening of Abbeylara Handball Sport & Social Centre and it was at this event that the effects of his illness were plain for all to see. While the trademark smile was still there, he was a man who "looked shook" as they say. His greying hair seemed to have become more grey, his voice was weak, though his handshake was strong and he had words for everyone before and after his speech.

Little did anyone know that within two weeks, he would have to resign his ministry – and that eleven weeks later he would be dead.

Chapter 10

End of an Era

I N APRIL 2008, BERTIE Ahern told a shocked cabinet meeting of his intention to resign the following month. This was greeted with some surprise and, according to some of those who were there, was also greeted with some tears. Séamus Brennan was not at that meeting due to his ill health, but that month was to prove to be an even more difficult one for Séamus.

His doctors advised him that his ongoing health problem required that he take a complete rest as his body appeared to be growing tired of all the stresses and strains in his life – and that necessitated retiring from Government. A letter to the Taoiseach-elect, Brian Cowen, was duly drafted and in early May before the new Taoiseach took over, Séamus formally announced his resignation as Minister for Arts, Sport and Tourism and that he would not be available to serve in Brian Cowen's administration. He would however continue to serve his constituents as TD for Dublin South and would not make any decision on the future until a general election arose.

In subsequent contacts with Brian Cowen, Séamus had indicated that if his health improved he hoped to be able to resume full duties in the future, including at cabinet or European level if the opportunity came up and the Taoiseach so decided. But it was not to be.

During the campaign for the Lisbon Treaty that year, the Taoiseach, accompanied by the Leader of the Labour Party, Eamon Gilmore, was visiting Dundrum Town Centre in the heart of the Dublin South constituency as part of his nationwide tour, and Séamus was determined to turn up to show solidarity with him and with Fianna Fáil. He did turn up to meet and greet Brian Cowen on his first official visit as Taoiseach to Dublin South, but it was clear to those present that this was a man who was very ill. After his death, the Taoiseach said he remembered "a brave and courageous man, exchanging words of encouragement upon my arrival and subsequently, the parting words, firm handshake and the inevitable smile that sought to reassure that all would be well".

But as he always did throughout his illness, Séamus made little of it and had time for everybody. One who met him was *Irish Times* journalist Harry McGee who wrote that "he was characteristically upbeat and positive and, as always asked me, a fellow Galwegian, how things were in Salthill and Glenard and Devon Park". McGee also recalled that even as his health was deteriorating, Séamus "still displayed the same ambition and appetite, though it was becoming more evident that this was a battle that he could not win."

When I met him for the last time, a few days before his death, he was heavily sedated, but he still had that disarming smile, the strong handshake, the warm greeting ("Hello, old friend"), and the inevitable question – "Do you want some food?" We chatted for a few minutes and he spoke of "the good times we had – and we will have more". But it was very clear that the end was not far away.

An illness which had been borne with great fortitude finally claimed Séamus Brennan on 9 July 2008, at the age of 60 years, four months and 23 days, barely two months after his resignation as Minister for Arts, Sport and Tourism, thus closing an illustrious Government career of nine ministries in 21 years, and a professional political life which covered 35 of what were among the most challenging years in Irish history.

During his short stint as Arts Minister, he had become very much at home with appropriate quotes from significant figures of the past and regularly used them in speeches. One of these was Rudyard Kipling, whose verses capture the very essence of what Séamus Brennan was about:

If you can keep your head when all about you
Are losing theirs and blaming it on you,
If you can trust yourself when all men doubt you
But make allowance for their doubting too,
If you can wait and not be tired by waiting,
Or being lied about, don't deal in lies,
Or being hated, don't give way to hating,
And yet don't look too good, nor talk too wise

If you can talk with crowds and keep your virtue
Or walk with kings--nor lose the common touch,
If neither foes nor loving friends can hurt you;
If all men count with you, but none too much,
If you can fill the unforgiving minute
With sixty seconds' worth of distance run,
Yours is the Earth and everything that's in it,
And – which is more – you'll be a Man, my son!

In the days and weeks following his death, numerous eulogies were spoken by friend and foe alike in public and in private. It was a real measure of his achievements that public figures and unknown constituents joined in the outpouring of grief at the loss of a significant figure in Irish life. The Chief Executive of Ryanair, Michael O'Leary, said that Séamus "was without doubt the most visionary Transport Minister that Ireland has ever had", a compliment which would not be so forthcoming for many of Séamus's political contemporaries. He added that low cost flights may not have existed across Europe if it was not for Séamus's courage in taking on vested interests to open up competition.

Among the many other tributes were the following:

"He played a major role in the building of the modern Ireland. His many talents were such that he could have been successful in several fields, yet it was a mark of the man that he chose to devote those gifts to public service and the public good. His achievements and contribution will leave a lasting mark on our country." – *Mary McAleese, President of Ireland*

"He served the nation and the Fianna Fáil Party with distinction. He was an astute and capable Minister who was interested in getting things done. He will be remembered as a brilliant political strategist, a dedicated constituency TD, a reforming Minister and a very popular colleague. He modernised the Party, making it a very skilled electoral machine. His achievements were many and they were of enormous consequence. He put his shoulder to the national wheel at a time when it would have been easier to sit on the sideline. Public Life was his vocation, and his one objective was to better the life of the people he served. He confronted his final battle with great fortitude and won the admiration of all his colleagues. Séamus's contribution will live on in the life of the nation." – *Brian Cowen, Taoiseach*

"He was a minister with impeccable judgement, great political instincts and a real appetite for hard work. I remember Séamus as a great force for calm in volatile days and someone I always got on personally extremely well with even when we differed politically on issues regarding direction and leadership of the party. I am deeply grateful for Séamus's unwavering support for me during my tenure as Leader of Fianna Fáil and as Taoiseach. Séamus was a brilliant colleague and a good friend. As Chief Whip, he did an outstanding job in my first Government which was a minority coalition Government supported by a number of independents. This Government was the first peace-time administration to complete a full Dáil term and Séamus's political skills were instrumental in this. It was my great pleasure to appoint Séamus as Minister for Transport, Minister for Social & Family Affairs and Minister for Arts, Sports and Tourism. In each of these departments,

Séamus made a lasting difference and his is a political legacy of positive change and true progress. Séamus has faced a serious illness with good grace and great courage." – *Bertie Ahern TD, former Taoiseach*

"Séamus brought a deep human understanding to all aspects of politics, and could always be relied upon to respond in a calm and measured way to any crisis. After Christmas, just outside these doors (Leinster House) he said to me: 'I've had a tough battle. I'm not sure whether I can weather this storm or not'. He has gone and politics is the poorer for his passing." – *Enda Kenny TD, Leader of Fine Gael*

"Modern politics can be a rough and sometimes brutal business but there was never a nasty word or phrase from Séamus Brennan. He was the essential political gentleman – a rare political phenomenon, a politician of strong convictions, effective for his party and quietly partisan, yet an extremely likeable person." – *Eamon Gilmore TD, Leader of the Labour Party.*

"He ran one of the most professional constituency organisations in the country and won the confidence of the electorate of Dublin South, time and time again." – *Mary Harney, TD, Minister for Health and Children*

In the months following, formal tributes were paid in special sessions of the Dáil and the Seanad where speakers from across the political divide vied with Independent Oireachtas Members to pay fulsome praise to what the Leader of the Seanad, Donie Cassidy, called "an exceptional figure in Irish public life".

It is worth noting some of the points made by other politicians in Leinster House:

"Séamus Brennan was a true professional who was greatly respected and loved by his constituents" – *Tom Kitt TD, Fianna Fáil*

"I always found Séamus to be a thorough gentleman in all his dealings. He will be a huge loss to Fianna Fáil and also I believe will be a loss to the Government in turbulent times as all could benefit from such calm confidence and ability." – *Eamon Ryan, TD, Minister for Communications, Energy and Natural Resources*

"His ability was beyond question in the many roles in which he served with distinction." – *Senator Ann Ormonde, Fianna Fáil*

"He was a true gentleman of politics and the constituency had a genuine, warm regard for him. There are many people whose life is better as a result of Séamus's assistance, and the untimely nature of his passing brings home to us the preciousness of life and the importance of valuing and making the most of every moment." – *Senator Maria Corrigan, Fianna Fáil*

"Ireland and Fianna Fáil will never be the same again without Séamus Brennan." – *Senator Mary White, Fianna Fáil*

"His legacy remains in every department in which he served and I regret that he was not left more often to do what came naturally to him, which was to reform." – *Senator Fiona O'Malley, Progressive Democrats*

"I got to know him very well when I was a Whip in the Opposition. He could not have been more generous with his time, and he facilitated me with any requests that were made. That established a relationship. He was a model of wisdom, courtesy, calmness, reliability and modesty. When he was Government Chief Whip and getting great press, I remember saying to him, 'Séamus, it seems that you are now a political star'. He said, 'John, there are no stars in politics'. It is a lesson we could usefully learn today. We are here to do a job and he did that job. He knew he was here to serve the public and he did that with total reliability, which was borne out by the fact that he topped the poll time and again. Sitting beside him in cabinet and watching him fight that illness was a difficult experience for all of us. He did so with great dignity. He never complained. He was a campaigning TD to the very last and served his constituents with total dedication." – *John Gormley TD, Minister for the Environment and Local Government and Leader of the Green Party*

"He brought common sense and clarity to every job he did." – *Eoin Ryan MEP, Fianna Fáil*

"As we all know, he was not a big man, but he had stature in his constituency." – *Olivia Mitchell TD, Fine Gael*

"He was courteous, affable and, highly importantly, always a man of his word" – *Caoimhghin Ó Caoláin TD, Sinn Féin*

"As a constituency rival, he was a completely trustworthy individual." – *Alan Shatter TD, Fine Gael*

"Séamus was an exemplary public representative. Regardless of where he served, Séamus earned the respect of colleagues on all sides of the House for his positive approach, courtesy and detailed grasp of the issues." – *Séamus Kirk TD, Fianna Fáil*

"Séamus was an outstanding politician, very decent and hard working. It was Séamus who, as General Secretary of Fianna Fáil in 1974, recommended the establishment of Ogra Fianna Fáil. It is the biggest youth wing of any political party in the country and it continues to go from strength to strength. Young people involved in politics of any persuasion today can thank Séamus Brennan for having the foresight to recognise their voice 34 years ago." – *Dara Calleary TD, Fianna Fáil*

"I am very sad at his passing. He was a very capable and courteous politician." – *Pat Rabbitte TD, former Labour Party Leader who also attended University College Galway with Séamus*

"To succeed in politics requires a certain temperament. Séamus met and exceeded this requirement." – *Senator Frances Fitzgerald, Fine Gael*

"He came to Fianna Fáil at a very appropriate time, just as we joined the European Union, and brought his Galway freshness – the fresh air of the west of Ireland. He lifted up the Party and was the essence of Fianna Fáil – and one of the important pillars." – *Dr. Michael Woods TD, Fianna Fáil*

"He had extraordinary skills of negotiation and mediation." – *Senator Joe O'Toole, Independent*

"One had to be up very early in the morning to catch Séamus out." – *Senator Dominic Hannigan, Labour*

"He was a natural leader, very attentive to his constituents. He brought new ideas and a new style as far as politics is concerned and was the complete politician." – *David Andrews TD, Fianna Fáil*

"He was probably single-handedly responsible for the introduction of modern campaigning techniques to Irish politics." – *Senator Dan Boyle, Green Party*

"Séamus Brennan had a rare combination of qualities that have been of immeasurable benefit to the people of Ireland. He was an extremely decent, warm, gentleman who had the capacity to bring people together and to encourage them to stay working with a common sense of purpose. And yet he was also a visionary Minister with superb organisational skills. Ireland has benefited from coalition governments and Séamus Brennan was at times the glue that held such governments together. And in his time as Minister, he was never a man to simply stick with the status quo. He was always seeking to change things for the better, sometimes with a bravery that is seldom seen in politics today." – *Senator Ciaran Cannon, Progressive Democrats*

"He was capable of rising above partisanship and being able to see the big picture." – *Senator Alex White, Labour*

"Séamus Brennan gave value for money. It was not enough to just put down a day's work but one had to bring something extra, something visionary, something passionate and something patriotic to it." – *Senator Eoghan Harris, Independent*

"If one approached him with a problem, it was not a matter of what he could *not* do for you but that he would *see* what could be done." – *Senator John Ellis, Fianna Fáil*

"He was a man of outstanding intelligence, tremendous ability and superb organisational skills. He brought a calmness and a positivity to all of the occasions and challenges and ultimate decisions that confronted him and Fianna Fail." – *Noel Treacy TD, Fianna Fáil*

"He had a forensic approach and he had something interesting to say." – *Senator Ronan Mullen, Independent*

"I saw how he listened to me and it impressed me as I rarely experienced it." – *Senator Fidelma Healy Eames, Fine Gael*

"He always joked that it was ironic that himself and Tom Kitt, who both hail from Galway, were TDs in Dublin South whereas I, a Dubliner, am a TD in Galway West." – *Éamon Ó Cuiv TD, Minister for Community, Rural and Gaeltacht Affairs*

"He was the most outstanding public representative this country has ever had." – *Senator Terry Leyden, Fianna Fáil*

"It came across always that Séamus was an extremely safe pair of hands on television and radio in any portfolio he held." – *Senator Pat Moylan, Cathaoirleach*

"This popular Galway man was a dedicated and indefatigable politician. Those of us who worked closely with him over the years through all his portfolios were always impressed by his intelligence, patience and his remarkable sense of judgment. He was a compassionate person with a great mind. A man of the deepest integrity, he was a colleague who was always available to give good advice" – *Martin Cullen TD, Minister for Arts, Sport and Tourism*

"Séamus was a gentleman, a politician of outstanding ability and a great diplomat." – *Dr. Rory O'Hanlon TD, Fianna Fáil*

"While he represented a Dublin constituency, Séamus was a native Galway man and he maintained a strong understanding of issues that affect rural Ireland. I found him to be one of the most accessible Ministers I have worked with."- *Pat the Cope Gallagher TD, Fianna Fáil*

"Séamus was one of the most influential figures in Cabinet. He carried out each of his portfolios with great wisdom, intelligence and understanding and he was widely regarded as being one of the great listeners of

Irish politics. He was always available for a good word or a piece of advice when needed and the great thing is that he never changed despite all his political success. He was always a gentleman and a real political grafter. The ultimate proof of that was how he continued to carry out his political duties until very recently, despite the serious nature of his illness. Up to the last he was the same old Séamus. The State has lost one of the greatest political figures of his generation." - *Brendan Kenneally TD, Fianna Fáil*

At his funeral in Holy Cross Church, Dundrum, attended by more than 1,000 mourners, his long time friend, Fr. Enda McDonagh, said that:

"... his family, constituents and friends have treasured him for so long, yet it was short, as Séamus died before his time. Today, we don't value life in the length of years, but rather what we have achieved in our time and, for Séamus, it has been a lot. We are here for the good of others. It's that kind of legacy we need to cherish in the name of Séamus Brennan."

Other comments:

"Always an innovative and creative Minister, he displayed considerable compassion and humanity. He was the consummate politician, skilled in the art of negotiation and respectful of alternative viewpoints. He brought an old-fashioned courtesy and charm to an often harsh and combative profession." – *Councillor Eibhlin Byrne, Lord Mayor of Dublin*

"It is no exaggeration to say that without Séamus Brennan's vision in the early 1980s, Ryanair would not exist today and the low fare air travel revolution which benefits so many millions of European citizens on a daily basis would have been strangled at birth." – *Michael O'Leary, Chief Executive, Ryanair*

"Séamus Brennan made a huge contribution to Irish aviation and was responsible for the liberalisation which the travelling public, both into and out of Ireland, has enjoyed for many years. When I took up the post three years ago I received a letter of great kindness and encouragement from Séamus Brennan, which I will never forget." – *Dermot Mannion, Chief Executive, Aer Lingus*

"Despite his diminutive status physically, he was a colossus." – *close friend Bob Manson Jr., on RTÉ Radio interview with Myles Dungan*

"He was a decent man and he will be missed." – *The Irish Times*

"He very clearly identified the real need to tackle child poverty during his tenure and raised its profile by regularly highlighting the issue. The problem of child poverty remains very much on today's political agenda due, in no small measure, to the work of Mr Brennan. The Alliance will always be grateful for his commitment to the issue and stands committed in carrying on his good work." – *Children's Rights Alliance*

"He was rare among Ministers in giving out his mobile number and even rarer in answering his calls personally, without the safety barrier of a private secretary or political minder. His briefings could often be heavy, providing worthy copy of the economics of politics with the astringency of the accountant that he was by profession. It was his misfortune never to have been Minister for Finance. Had illness and early death not ordained otherwise, Séamus Brennan would have been a wise and cool head in the difficult economic days facing

Brian Cowen's disarrayed Ministerial team." – *John Cooney, Irish Independent*

"A shrewd but gentle political operator who was undoubtedly one of the Dáil's good guys, he was one of the nation's most popular politicians whose shrewd perceptiveness, warm gentle manner and political brain set him apart in the normally dull world of Irish politics. No matter what the occasion, he listened, he was gracious with his time, and he managed to make those in his company feel important." – *Daniel McConnell, Sunday Independent*

"He frequently adopted an imaginative and innovative approach to problems." – *Brendan Keenan, Irish Independent*

"His concern was not restricted to economic and commercial development. He had a wide range of ideas, was an excellent listener, sought views from many people and had interests outside the narrow and introverted circle of the public service – a trait he shared with the late Sean Lemass, and despite their well publicised differences, George Colley and Charlie Haughey." – *Letter to the Editor, Irish Independent, from Ronald Phelan, Cabinteely*

"Minister Brennan leaves a long and distinguished list of achievements behind him. He served two terms as Minister for Transport where he earned the respect and admiration of the AA." – *Automobile Association*

"Séamus Brennan had all the political qualities. He had vision, ambition and determination. He was single minded and had the necessary application. He was organised. He enjoyed the status of 'nice guy'. He was courteous, polite and mannerly. He was bright, crafty and had all the social skills. He knew how things worked.

He was street wise from early on. He was the consummate performer, whether in parliament or the media. He was a negotiator, an innovator, fixer, healer, dealer and wheeler. He was a decent man, a good man, a kind man, he worked very hard, he mattered, he made a difference." – *Ralph O'Gorman, Galway Independent*

"His time as Minister for Arts, Sport and Tourism showed his characteristic determination, innovation and zeal for progress and understanding." – *Dermot McLoughlin, Chief Executive, Temple Bar Cultural Trust*

"He was our Minister for the Arts for just a short period, but in that time, as in all the other Ministerial positions he held over the years, he took to the task with great energy and brought a wealth of experience to the job. He started from day one by meeting us, and assuring us that he was totally committed to working with us for the good of the arts and of artists." – *Olive Braiden, Chair of the Arts Council*

"In the many engagements which have taken place between our administrations, I have always found Séamus to be someone with whom real progress could be made on issues of significant benefit to our people." – *Martin McGuinness MLA, Deputy First Minister of Northern Ireland*

"This news comes with a great sense of sadness to all who knew and worked with Séamus. I always found him to be a responsible, dedicated and responding Minister. He was always co-operative in North–South matters and was a man of strong political beliefs and social conscience. Unfortunately, Séamus has had to endure sickness for some time now and his loss will be keenly felt by his family and all those who worked with him and those he worked for." – *Pat Ramsey MLA, SDLP*

Culture, Arts and Leisure Spokesperson, Northern Ireland Assembly

"His commitment to the tourist industry and desire to make a difference was evident in everything which he did, as was his keen understanding of all relevant issues. Throughout his Ministerial career, his support and engagement was pivotal in shaping the direction of Irish transport and tourism, particularly in light of the challenges confronted by the sector." – *Matthew Ryan, President, Irish Hotels Federation*

"He undoubtedly took pleasure in allocating funding of €1.2 million towards the development of a new Arts Centre and Theatre in Ballina, given his close personal links with the North Mayo capital. He had spent time here in the 1960s during his career in accountancy and was a well known face in the *Western People* offices on Kevin Barry Street where he audited the accounts for his Dublin based employers, O'Connor Accountants." – *Western People*

"All of Ireland is better off as a result of his contributions as a TD and Minister." – *Michael Sanfey, President, Dun Laoghaire Rathdown Chamber*

"There is an Irish saying, 'Ní bheidh a leithéid ann arís', meaning we shall never see his likes again. It could be written for Séamus Brennan. In what can be termed the great pool of politics, he shone out like no one else. He was different, human, caring and humorous. He had a smile when smiles were rare on the faces of politicians. His smile came from a place that many politicians rarely entered – the very heart of the being." – *Liamy MacNally, Mayo News*

"He could always walk in other people's shoes and consider situations from their perspective." – *Martina Devlin, Irish Independent*

"In Séamus's all too brief tenure as Minister for Arts, Sports and Tourism, I found him courteous, understanding and helpful." – *Nickey Brennan, President of the GAA*

"We valued him as a graduate and also as a talented politician who served his country with complete commitment." – *Dr. James Brown, President of NUI Galway*

"Normally people like to say nice things about someone when they die. But even by that standard, the tributes to Séamus Brennan were extraordinary." – *Irish Examiner*

"A decent and honourable man who had vision and foresight. As Minister for Transport, he listened carefully to the views of community and political leaders as a result of which the Western Rail Corridor is currently being developed in line with the National Spatial Strategy as part of Transport 21. The people of the West, who will benefit enormously from that initiative for years to come, will warmly remember him." – *West on Track Campaign*

"His ten Ministerial successes flew in the face of the old maxim that politics is no place for a gentleman." – *Sam Smyth, Irish Independent*

"Ireland was lucky to have such a man – talented, hard-working and honourable – this country deserves more politicians like Séamus Brennan." – *Shane Coleman, Sunday Tribune*

"He achieved far more than most politicians; however, the fact that he didn't become Taoiseach meant he never fulfilled his true potential. There is almost universal recognition that he was an honourable politician and a decent man who did the State some service. Not a bad legacy to leave behind." – *Andrew Lynch, Evening Herald*

Tributes from Blogs

"He was a nice man, which isn't necessarily a default comment for politicians. I never saw a trace of spite or aggression or superiority in him. He was kind, self-deprecating and extremely civil – in a non-patronising way – to his political opponents" – *Irish Times columnist Sarah Carey on her blogging website, GUBU*

"Séamus always had an open door and a willing ear for a logical argument. He did much to open up the aviation market into and out of Ireland and was very active in promoting Ireland as a destination notwithstanding the illness he was fighting" – *Travelwise, the Irish Travel Agents Association blog*

"I don't think I'll break with tradition.
I will not speak ill of the dead.
Poor Séamus was some politician.
And that's all that needs to be said.

Whatever my personal viewpoint,
(I'm just a mere critical knave)
It isn't worth making a new point
'Bout someone so fresh in the grave.

In life, I was always quite critical –
It serves little use to deny it –
But now one should not be political.
'Tis seemlier now to keep quiet."

– *Peter Goulding, Pete's political Verse*

"Around the time he was dithering between the PDs and FF, I had not much time for him. However, as Minister for Social Affairs he grew on me and seemed to have a lot of good positive things to say." *–Anonymous*

"Met him once, seemed like a nice fella. I remember thinking: 'bad hair, very short, but not a bad ol feicer all the same'," *– Anonymous*

"Hard to believe he will not be seen on the News/Questions and Answers, etc. anymore." *– Anonymous*

"I always thought he came across as an intelligent, considered man and in the late 70s early 80s, I thought he would be Taoiseach one day. He possibly had all the attributes except the ruthless streak, which is to his credit also. His stand against Charlie Haughey (with the gang of 22) confirmed his integrity for me." *– Anonymous*

"Never did I ever hear him give cheap digs or peevish replies to opposition spokespeople or the media but he was nevertheless an effective and determined minister. A proud Fianna Fáil man of the old breed and a proud Galway man who never forgot his roots." *– Anonymous*

"Really decent man. The higher up he went, the less he appeared to give a s...e what people thought of him. He seemed to have political beliefs that he followed through on, which is rare in this country." *– Anonymous*

"He was his own man and one that kept his integrity intact while many of his colleagues drowned in their failings. The government will miss his skills and experience – the country will miss his decency." *– Anonymous*

"We have lost a giant." – *Anonymous*

"I know nothing about his politics but I was always eager
to see him on telly." – *Anonymous*

These quotes represent just a tiny flavour of what was spoken
and written about Séamus Brennan following his untimely death.
At times like this, it is easy for some people to forget the grief suffered by non-family members who have also suffered a loss – their
boss, their colleague and, more significantly, their friend who was
with them day in and day out, in the good times and the bad times.
Ireland will indeed be a very different place without Séamus, but
his work lives on as testimony to a consummate politician whom
the journalist and author John Cooney described as "a backroom
genius with front-of-house charm".

And as columnist Andrew Lynch pointed out in the TheHer-
ald.ie: "Sadly he never got to enjoy the retirement that he'd promised himself for so long."

Séamus was a rare human being with charisma, character,
honesty and friendliness whose mould was broken after he was
created. It was a privilege to have known him in this life.

The well known words of poet Laurence Binyon (1869-1943),
from his poem "For the Fallen", will have a resonance for all who
knew, or just admired, Séamus Brennan:

> They shall grow not old, as we that are left grow old.
> Age shall not weary them, nor the years condemn.
> At the going down of the sun and in the morning,
>   We will remember them.

Ar dheis Dé go raibh a ainm.

Appendix 1

Milestones and Notable Achievements

Milestones

- Member of Dáil Éireann (11 June 1981 – 9 July 2008)
- Member of Seanad Éireann (27 October 1977 – 11 June 1981)
- General Secretary of Fianna Fáil (1973 – 1979)
- Minister for Trade and Marketing (10 March 1987 – 12 July 1989)
- Minister for Tourism and Transport (12 July 1989 – 7 February 1991)
- Minister for Tourism, Transport and Communications (7 February 1991 – 11 February 1992)
- Minister for Education (11 February 1992 – 12 January 1993)
- Minister for Commerce and Technology (12 January 1993 – 15 December 1994)
- Front Bench Spokesman on Transport, Energy and Communications (15 December 1994 – 6 June 1997)
- Government Chief Whip, Minister of State at the Department of the Taoiseach and at the Department of Defence (26 June 1997 – 6 June 2002)
- Minister for Transport (6 June 2002 – 29 September 2004)

- Minister for Social and Family Affairs (29 September 2004 – 14 June 2007)

- Minister for Arts, Sport & Tourism (14 June 2007 – 6 May 2008)

Notable Achievements

- **As Minister for Trade and Marketing:** The first Minister to have this role, he brought all his political skills to bear on a new way for promoting business and developing the economy – the early days of the Celtic Tiger.

- **As Minister for Tourism, Transport and Communications:** Began the work on what was subsequently to become the Luas, following up on his work as a Member of Seanad Éireann to have the old Harcourt Street Railway reopened for public transport; instituted a two-airline national policy which made air travel from Ireland more accessible to all.

- **As Minister for Education:** Published the Green Paper on Education which placed special emphasis on giving priority to disadvantaged students and charted the way forward for several successive Ministers.

- **As Minister for Commerce and Technology:** Established the Task Force on Small Business which gave official recognition to small business with the unique distinction of having recommendations acted on in advance of the formal Report from the Task Force.

- **As Government Chief Whip and Minister of State at Defence:** Successfully steered the first ever full term coalition Government for the maximum period of five years; chaired the National Millennium Committee which brought the Millennium message to every village and town in Ireland, including the delivery of a Millennium Candle to every household and the planting of a tree for every family; initiated and steered the legislation to give Civil Defence a statutory role.

- **As Minister for Transport:** Completed work on the roll out of the Luas (which he had first instigated back in 1979 as a Member of Seanad Éireann); introduced Penalty Points which have had a significant effect on driver behaviour – and saved lives; provided funding to roll out the national motorway network linking the cities; dramatically improved the availability of taxis; and began work on what subsequently became the Garda Traffic Corps.

- **As Minister for Social & Family Affairs:** Abolished "old age" by removing the term from pension payments; negotiated increased payments to the elderly and the most vulnerable; began work on encouraging and facilitating social welfare recipients to be more active without losing their payments; and successfully steered the debate on the importance of pension provision.

- **As Minister for Arts, Sport and Tourism:** Oversaw important and strategic developments in all policy areas, including making the arts more accessible to all, developing the opportunities for more participation in all sports, and providing the framework for generating more tourism.

New Boards Appointed by Séamus Brennan

National Marketing Group (constituted 1988): Minister Séamus Brennan (Chairman); John Burns, Managing Director, Birex Pharmaceuticals Ltd; Prof. Anthony Cunningham, Department of Marketing, UCD; David Dand, Chairman and Managing Director, Gilbey's of Ireland Sales Ltd.; Mark Kavanagh, Managing Director, Hardwicke Ltd.; Howard Kilroy, President and Chief Operations Director, Jefferson Smurfit Group Ltd.; Liam Kilroy, Principal Officer, Office of Trade and Marketing; David Kingston, Managing Director, Irish Life Assurance Company; Alan McCarthy, Chief Executive, Córas Tráchtála/Irish Export Board; Alan McDonnell, Marketing Manager, Superquinn and former Chairman of the Marketing Institute of Ireland; Aidan McKenna, Chief Executive, Memory Computer Ltd.; Joe Moran, Chairman, Irish Wire plc; Vivian Murray, Chief Executive, Irish Goods Council; Eugene O'Neill, independent businessman; Dermot Ryan, Managing Director, O'Flaherty Holdings Ltd.; John Ryan, Sales and Marketing Manager, Leo Laboratories.

Task Force on Small Business (constituted 1993): Minister Séamus Brennan (Chairman); Seamus Butler, Butler Manufacturing Services Ltd.; Oliver Cleary, Gercon Enginering and Development Ltd.; Des Cummins, Cummins Metal Recycling Ltd.; Alan Elliott, Ano-Terchnology Ltd.; Peter Faulkner, Faulkner Export Packaging Ltd.; Audrey Glynn, G & M Industrial Cleaning Products; Sean Hannick, Killala Precision Components Ltd.; Val Keating, Caraplas; William Loughnane, County Arms Hotel; Carmel Lynch, Procut Enginering Processes Ltd.; Brian McHale, Precision Alarm Ltd.; Des McWilliam, McWilliam Sailmakers Ltd.; Louis Mulcahy, Potadoireacht na Caoloige; Lorraine Sweeney, L S Catering Ltd.; John Corcoran, Department of Enterprise and Employment; Dick Doyle, Economic Adviser to the Minister.

National Millennium Committee (constituted 1998): Minister Séamus Brennan (Chairman); Joe Barry, former Director-General of RTE; Peter Barry, former Fine Gael Government Minister; Eithne Healy, Chair of Dublin Theatre Festival; Richard Holland, Principal Officer in the Department of the Taoiseach; Ronan Keating, Boyzone; Derek Keogh, Chair of Millennium Festivals Ltd.; Howard Kilroy, Governor, Bank of Ireland Group; Paul McGuinness, Manager of U2; Monica McWilliams, Northern Ireland Women's Coalition; Brian Murphy, Chairman of the Office of Public Works; Patricia O'Donovan, Deputy Secretary, Irish Congress of Trades Union; Deirdre Purcell, author and journalist; Lochlainn Quinn, Chairman, Allied Irish Banks Group.

Civil Defence Board (constituted 2002): Dr. Michael Ryan (Chairman); Councillor Paddy Durack, Thurles Urban District Council; Councillor Margaret Adams, Mayo County Council; Councillor Tony Kelly, Dun Laoghaire-Rathdown County Council; Gerry Gervin, Civil Defence Headquarters; Ned Gleeson, Limerick County Manager; Sean Hogan, Senior Fire Adviser; Dr. Ann McGarry, Chief Executive Officer, Radiological Protection Institute of Ireland; Irene O'Meara, Instructor, Civil Defence Headquarters; Declan Burns, former Deputy Director General, Environmental Protection Agency; Michael Fitzsimons, former Chairman, Civil Defence Officers Association; Commandant Kevin Houston, Director of Engineering, Defence Forces; Chief Superintendent John T. Farrelly, Garda National Traffic Bureau; Frances Moynihan, Civil Defence Volunteer, Waterford.

Taxi Advisory Council (constituted 2003): Pat Byrne (Chairman); Chief Superintendent Denis Fitzpatrick, Garda Sioch-ána; Noreen Mackey, Competition Authority; Sadie Doherty, consumer and community interests; Jerry Brennan, SIPTU; John Ussher, Irish Taxi Drivers Federation; Deirdre Power, Irish Hotels Federation; Deirdre O'Keeffe, Failte Ireland; Michael Kilcoyne, Consumers Association of Ireland; Vincent Kearns, National Taxi Drivers Union; Denise Kinahan, Taxi Company Owners Association; Tom Fannin, National Chauffeur Drive Association; Brian Killeen, Transport Logistics; Mary Keogh, National Disability Authority; Vincent Thornton, Irish Motor Industry; Carmel Mulroy, Chambers of Commerce of Ireland; Christopher Humphrey, National Private Hire & Taxi Association; Joe Gavin, County & City Managers Association.

Dublin Airport Authority (constituted 2004): Gary McGann (Chairman), Chief Executive Officer of the Jefferson Smurfit Group and a former Chief Executive Officer of Aer Lingus; Sir Michael Hodgkinson, former Chief Executive of the British Airport Authority; Colm Barrington, international aviation expert with 35 years experience in the industry and former Chief Executive of aircraft leasing firm, Guinness Peat Aviation; Marie O'Connor, Audit Partner in Pricewaterhouse Coopers and Barrister; Bill Cullen, Chairman and Owner of Renault Ireland; Anthony Spollen, International Internal Audit Expert and former senior executive in AIB Bank; Desmond Cummins, Chairman of the Cummins Group and former Member of the Government Task Force on Small Business; Mary Davis, National Director, Special Olympics Ireland.

Shannon Airport Authority (constituted 2004): Patrick Shanahan (Chairman), Chief Executive, Atlantic Technology Corridor and former Managing Director, Tellabs Ltd.; Patrick Blaney, Chief Executive, Blackstream Aviation and former Chief Executive, AerFi Group plc and Guinness Peat Aviation; Rose Hynes, Aviation Lawyer, former Aer Lingus Board Member, former Guinness Peat Aviation executive and board member of several companies; Tadhg Kearney, Chairman, Air Transport Users Council; Michael B. Lynch, Group Managing Director, Lynch Hotel Group, and former Young Entrepreneur of the Year; Padraic Burke, corporate finance expert with commercial, retail and investment interests in Galway, Dublin and Britain; Reg Freake, Senior Executive of Dell Group, former Managing Director, Dell Canada, and former aviation specialist in Canadian Air Traffic Control; Olivia Loughnane, Communications, Research & Development Director of Shannon Development Company and former EU Commission official.

Cork Airport Authority (constituted 2004): Joe Gantly, Chairman, former Managing Director for European Operations, Apple Computers; Pat Dalton, Chief Financial Officer, Bord Gais, former Group Chief Accountant Guinness Peat Aviation, and former Chief Financial Officer, GPA/debis AirFinance Group; Loretta Glucksman, Chairwoman, American Ireland Fund; Humphry Murphy, Director, Global Stainless Ltd. and Chairman, Hygienic Stainless Steels based in Britain; Don Cullinane, Chief Executive, Beacon Travel Group; Alf Smiddy, Managing Director, Beamish & Crawford plc and former Chartered Accountant with Pricewaterhouse Coopers; Veronica Perdisatt, Chairwoman, Kilkenny Group and former Vice-President of EMC Group based in Ovens, Co. Cork; Eoin Ó Cathain, Managing Director, Ó Cathain Iasc Teoranta, international businessman and former official with AIB Bank.

Appendix 3

Did You Know ...?

- Séamus Brennan was succeeded by Martin Cullen in his final three Ministerial portfolios – Transport; Social and Family Affairs; Arts, Sport and Tourism.

- Before Martin Cullen, the last three Ministers for Arts, Sport and Tourism have held that portfolio as their last Cabinet appointment – Jim McDaid, John O'Donoghue and Séamus Brennan.

- Séamus Brennan was just 25 when he became General Secretary of Fianna Fáil, thus beginning his professional political life, and became a Senator at 29, a TD at 33 and a Minister at 39.

- As General Secretary of Fianna Fáil, Séamus (along with Senator Eoin Ryan) was the person who gave Bertie Ahern his start in the Dáil by adding him as a candidate for the 1977 General Election after Bertie narrowly lost out at a selection convention for the Dublin-Finglas Constituency.

- Séamus was the first Member of the Oireachtas to open a full-time Constituency Office – when he was a Senator in 1979, first at 3 Landscape Road, Churchtown and then at 9 Braemor Road, Churchtown.

- Brennan's Yard Hotel in Galway City, which was officially opened by Séamus as Minister for Tourism, was originally the location for the building business of James Brennan, Séamus's father.

- Séamus Brennan used to drive rally cars when he was young.

- His birthday is two days after St. Valentine's Day (February 16).

- A website called thefreedictionary.com has an acronym for "Séamus" – "**S**ociety for **E**lectro-**A**coustic **M**usic in the **U**nited **S**tates.

- An actor called Michael Bell played a character called Séamus Brennan in "Ironside –Murder Impromptu" in 1971.

- Séamus Brennan played golf – but he was not the Séamus Brennan who came third in the Pattaya Sports Club Annual Golf Championship at the Plutaluang Royal Thai Naval Course, Thailand in 2003.

- His official golf handicap was hovering around 18 or 19, but those who played with him often felt it should have been more like 10 or 12.

- One time on an official visit to the United States, Séamus was asked by a television presenter if he knew that the programme was going out coast-to-coast – his reply was that when he appeared on Irish television, it went coast-to-coast also!

- Séamus was a passionate supporter of West Ham Football Club.

- Before attaining Ministerial office, he was an accountant and management consultant.

- His maternal uncle, Charles O'Donnell from Letterkenny, said that he gave Séamus his first lesson in economics. As a young person, Séamus often visited Letterkenny where Uncle Charlie owned a bakery. Séamus helped out and was paid for his labours. On the first pay day, Uncle Charlie put out the money due to Séamus on the table and Séamus was delighted. However, Uncle Charlie proceeded to count out deductions for food, bed, electricity, etc., which left very little for the poor

Séamus to spend as he wished but gave him an invaluable economic lesson.

- He went to lots of piano lessons as a child – but could only ever play one piece of music, "The Dear Little Shamrock", which he practised relentlessly much to the annoyance of his siblings.

- He took Irish dancing lessons as a child and while he could do Irish dancing very well, he found it difficult to do so without holding on to a table or a chair.

- He never learnt to swim – despite being a member of Galway Swimming Club for many years and the best efforts of swimming coach, Jimmy Cranny.

- Séamus was "known to the Gardai" – at age 5. He wandered off from a family group in Letterkenny, Co. Donegal and was found out of the town by a passing truck driver who alerted the Gardai and reunited him with his family.

- He used to love occasional boating trips on the Shannon – but never liked to be away for longer than a week or two on holidays.

- When visiting a foreign Ambassador one time, Séamus was reminded by his Private Secretary to sympathise with the Ambassador whose mother had recently passed away: "Sorry to hear you buried your mother," said Séamus, to which the Ambassador replied with a very straight face, "I had to, Minister, she was dead."

- When playing golf with his brother, Terry, Séamus was a regular winner of their IR£5 bets, and one time he insisted on paying the winnings in full public view in the bar after the game. This was to show people that he was the winner and greatly enhanced his enjoyment of defeating his brother!

- He was the holder of three degrees: B.Comm and B.A. (Econ.) from University College Galway, and M.Comm from University College Dublin.

- He studied entirely through the Irish language for his degrees at University College Galway.

- He once accepted a lift from Naas Road to Leinster House after his car broke down – only strange thing is that the lift was in a dumper truck (thanks to Jackie Boardman).

- As a Galway man representing a Dublin Constituency, he had a real difficulty in deciding who to shout for when the two teams met – but he always said that there were lots of Galway people in Dublin South.

- When dining with a number of Scandanavian Ambassadors, he was presented with a bowl of snails as the first course – he spent the time moving them around the bowl but not eating them as they looked just like the snails which populated his back garden.

- Among the many people who shared the name Séamus Brennan are the Chief Accounting Officer for Analog Devices; the Chief Executive Officer of CUSP Point Software Ltd., Gaelic footballers for Meath (1966) and Kilkenny (2009); the Project Coordinator for Churches Acting Together (USA); a Catholic priest in Somerville, Massachusetts; a Scottish rugby player; an under-14 hurling champion in Tipperary (2002) and a Manchester United fullback (also known as Shay) up to 1970.

About the Author

Frank Lahiffe studied law and public relations and has held positions in advertising, marketing, public relations and journalism. He was appointed by successive Governments as adviser to Séamus Brennan throughout an entire Government career which spanned 21 years (1987–2008) across nine Government departments.

The personal relationship between Frank and Séamus goes back to 1980 when the latter, as a member of Seanad Éireann, was a candidate for the first of nine successful general election campaigns (and one local election campaign) after he had resigned as Fianna Fáil General Secretary in 1979. They shared numerous secrets as they worked their joint way through the various Government departments, but many of those secrets must remain confidential due to the Official Secrets Act.

But their links to each other and to Fianna Fáil go back even farther. Frank's late uncle and Godfather, Robert Lahiffe from Gort, was Fianna Fáil TD for South Galway under Eamon de Valera and served in Seanad Éireann under Sean Lemass. His maternal grandfather, John J. Shiel from Woodford, was a Fianna Fáil Councillor. Séamus's late father, James Brennan, was Director of Elections for Fianna Fáil in South Galway, although he was originally from Roscommon where Séamus's paternal grandfather was also a prominent figure in Fianna Fáil.

After leaving Government service on the retirement of Séamus Brennan, Frank went on to become a Public Affairs Consultant with his own business, Lahiffe & Associates, Public Affairs and Political Communications.

Index